Longman
practice kit

GCSE
Mathematics

Brian Speed

6th June
13th June

LONGMAN

SERIES EDITORS
Geoff Black and Stuart Wall

TITLES AVAILABLE
GCSE
Biology
Business Studies
Chemistry
English
French
Geography
German
Higher Level Mathematics
Information Technology
Mathematics
Physics
Science

A-level
Biology
British and European Modern History
Business Studies
Chemistry
Economics
French
Geography
German
Mathematics
Physics
Psychology
Sociology

Addison Wesley Longman Ltd.,
Edinburgh Gate, Harlow,
Essex CM20 2JE, England
and Associated Companies throughout the World.

© Addison Wesley Longman 1997

First published 1997
Second Impression 1997

ISBN 0582-30385-0

British Library Cataloguing-in-Publication Data
A catalogue record for this book is available from the British Library.

Set by 32 in 11/13pt Baskerville
Produced by Longman Singapore Publishers Pte Ltd
Printed in Singapore

Contents

How to use this book

This book seeks to help you achieve a good grade in your GCSE Mathematics examination. It covers core topics which are common to all exam boards and some other topics that are very likely to be on your syllabus.

The book is arranged in four parts.

Part I Preparing for the examination

This section covers what you should be doing before and during the examination. It gives some helpful advice on planning your revision and using examination questions in revision. A revision planner is provided with this book to help you structure your revision beginning some weeks before the examination. There is also an explanation of the different sorts of examination question and the key words that you are likely to find in examination questions to help you understand the questions that are set. Finally there is some advice for the actual examination day.

Part II Topic areas, summaries and questions

This section has been split into eight key topic areas which have been chosen to give you essential information to make your revision easier. In each area you will find:

1 **Topic outline and revision tips** These will not replace your own full notes but will give you most of the basic facts that you need, with plenty of examples, and they present the material in a short fact form that is easier to revise. If you need more detail the *Longman Study Guide Mathematics* and the *Longman Study Guide Higher Mathematics* are good sources.
2 **Revision activity** Making revision active is one of the best ways to improve your understanding. Once you have tried these short examples to the best of your ability, look at the answers in Part III.
3 **Practice questions** The examination questions at the end of each topic are designed to test your knowledge of the topic area. It will help you to judge whether you need to spend more time revising that topic. Fill in the answers in the spaces provided. Again, do make sure that you try to answer the questions before you look up the answers in part III. Don't give up too easily or you aren't making the best use of the questions!

Part III Answers and grading

Here you will find answers to the revision activities and practice questions, with details of the grading. Use these to check your answers *after* you have attempted to answer the questions.

Part IV Timed practice papers

This section contains a series of examination questions covering a variety of topics to give you practice in timing yourself under exam-type conditions before the examination. Outline answers are provided after each examination paper for you to check your performance. Use the grading schemes outlined at the start of this section.

part I

Preparing for the Examination

Planning your revision

- ▶ Start revising in good time. There is a lot to revise, and if you leave it too late, you will make it very difficult for yourself.
- ▶ Try to give a set amount of revision time to Mathematics each week; this ought to fit into a general timetable to give yourself time to revise all your subjects. Mathematics is best revised in short bursts.
- ▶ Make sure you know what is in the Intermediate Mathematics syllabus and what is in the Higher Mathematics syllabus; there is no point learning things that will not appear in the examination. This book supports the Intermediate Level but it is a vital foundation for work at the Higher Level.
- ▶ Make sure you have looked at the whole of your Mathematics syllabus and have broken it down into the topics you will revise, so you know what you are going to revise and when.
- ▶ If you get really stuck on a topic then have a break – do something else and come back to this topic maybe the next day (don't forget it all together because it won't go away!). You will find that the more times you visit a topic to revise it, the clearer it becomes. Pennies start to drop, as they say.
- ▶ You will not find it very productive just to read your maths revision books. You must get actively engaged, for example by doing some Mathematics problems. The best way to revise Mathematics is to do problems for which you have worked solutions. You can then check yourself against these solutions to find whether or not you are right and get help if you are stuck.
- ▶ Practise answering examination questions under exam conditions if you can. There are timed examination questions at the end of this book that are very useful in this respect. After all, it is this timed situation that you are preparing yourself for.
- ▶ Don't expect revising to be easy. Mathematics is the most difficult subject to learn; there are very few people who find it easy, so don't get anxious when you find the going is tough – stick at it and use this book to help build up your confidence and knowledge. Most of your friends will be finding revising Mathematics difficult too.

Examination questions in revision

After you have revised a topic, it is important that you try the examination questions in that topic area. You will find a revision activity in each part of the book to help you learn the basic topic work, but then you need to try the practice questions to get used to the examination language and format. There are full explanations at the back of the book about the common errors you could have made, as well as a breakdown as to how you score marks for each part of the question.

Trying these practice questions has many advantages:

- ▶ It will let you know whether you have understood the topic or not.
- ▶ Any difficulties will soon become apparent and you will have time to do something about it before getting into the examination room.
- ▶ You will start to recognise those types of question that you know you can do well, and those that you know you have to exercise great care over.
- ▶ You will become familiar with the language that is used for many examination questions.
- ▶ When you look at the full solution you will see whether you have managed to answer the question in the way the examiner intends.
- ▶ The timed examination questions at the end of the book will prepare you for working to strict times in the examination.

► Your confidence will be boosted by realising how many examination questions you can actually answer, and of course this will improve every time you use the book.

Types of examination question

In Mathematics there are a few different types of question. These are described below.

Short questions
At the start of the examination, and at the start of some longer questions, you have short questions designed to test just one single thing.

Example
Solve $5x + 6 = 17$

This is a short question and involves solving an equation and you will see that you will score either 1 or 2 marks for this type of question.

Structured questions
Structured questions are long questions that develop some idea and use earlier answers to help do the later parts.

Example
At an Outdoor Centre the water storage tank is a cuboid of dimensions 2 m by 1m by 1.5 m.
(a) Calculate the volume of the water storage tank.

The mugs at the Centre are all cylindrical with a radius of 4 cm and a height of 9 cm.

(b) How much water does a full mug hold?

The Warden at the Centre claimed that from one full tank, you get over 6 000 full mugs of water.

(c) Is he correct ? Show all your working.

The two first parts of this structured question are just like two short questions, but you need both these answers to be able to answer part (c). It is written like this to help you work towards the final part. This link is not always there, but in a longer question there is usually a link between the parts.

Non-structured questions
Non-structured questions are usually thought to be the most difficult, because you are given a problem and you have to find your own way through it without the guidance of part questions along the way.

Example
Key Soup is canned by a small family business. Each morning the family makes 200 litres of soup. This is put into cylindrical tins each of which is 8.4 cm high and has a diameter of 7 cm.
How many of these tins can be filled from the 200 litres of soup?

The question can be answered only after you have worked out the volume of a tin, changed litres to cubic centimetres and then divided. First, though, you had to see for yourself what you needed to find out.

Reason questions
There are reason questions, where you have to give some explanation or a description of a situation and not just provide a calculation.

Example
The school bus should pick up Joseph at 8.50 a.m. each school morning.
Sometimes the bus is not on time.
Describe how Joseph could estimate the probability of this bus being late.

A description is wanted as to how you would attempt to solve this problem, and not just a calculation to data that has been given.

It is most likely that you will find this type of question in the data handling questions, but it may occur elsewhere too.

Drawing questions

There are always questions where you either have to construct a diagram with ruler and compass, or where you have to draw a net or a graph.

All of these questions will require an accuracy of being less than 1 millimetre out in your measurement. If angles are involved then you are normally expected to be no more than 2° out.

Command Words used in the Examination

▶ **Write down**   you do not need to do any calculation, the answer is simple!
▶ **Calculate**   you do need to do some calculation to find the answer.
▶ **Find**   you may have to do some simple calculation, but not as much as if the question said 'calculate'.
▶ **What is**   this means the same as find.
▶ **Explain**   you need to show very clearly how you arrive at the answer.
▶ **Draw**   you can use a ruler, protractor or anything else you want to produce the diagram.
▶ **Construct**   you cannot use a protractor, only a ruler and compass (of course, a pencil too).
▶ **Use your graph to**   the answer is to be found by following a particular line on the graph.
▶ **Approximately**   you must give a rounded answer, and a sensible rounding that will probably be an integer (whole number) or to the nearest thousand; it all depends on the context of the question.

During the examination

Remember:
▶ The examiners ask questions on your syllabus only, so you have seen all these questions before.
▶ If you have forgotten how to do it, leave it and come back to it. Do what you can do well first.
▶ Read every question at least twice – it's a shame to answer the wrong question, because you don't get as many marks.
▶ Show your working out because the examiners give marks for the method being correct even if the answer is wrong.
▶ Look at the number of marks for each question, it's a hint as to how much is involved and how much time to spend on the question. 1 mark per minute, is a 'rule of thumb' which is easy to remember, but it's only a guide.
▶ Don't stop – even when you've finished the paper. Remember that you are most unlikely to get every question right, so check back to find any errors you might have made and do something about it. You have only the time in the exam to demonstrate all the mathematics you have learnt, so don't waste that time.
▶ Learn from Paper 1 to Paper 2; if some major topics have been well covered in Paper 1 its unlikely that they will reappear on Paper 2. So be wise: think about what now might be on Paper 2 once you have seen Paper 1.

part II

Topic areas, and practice questions

Number

In revising the topic of number you are dealing with the basics of numeracy that will occur throughout your examination. You will only be asked once to perform certain skills, but there are those like rounding off and percentage that will occur quite a few times on every exam paper. You need to be very familiar with these topics or you can lose a lot of marks.

Number outline revision

Long multiplication

To work out 546×37, you would do

```
    546
×    37
  3 822    (546 multiplied by 7 )
 16 380    (546 multiplied by 30)
 20 202    (the two added together)
```

Long division

Example

How many coaches holding 42 people each will be needed to take a school party of 543?

We read the problem and realise that we have to do a division: $543 \div 42$

```
        12
  42 ⟌ 543
        42
       123
        84
        39
```

The answer is that there will be 12 full coaches and one coach with 39 passengers.
So there will be a need to book 13 coaches.

Fractions of quantities

Example

Find $\frac{3}{5}$ of £235

Find $\frac{1}{5}$ first by dividing by 5, then find $\frac{3}{5}$ by multiplying by 3, i.e.

$235 \div 5 = 47$

then $47 \times 3 = £141$

Negative number arithmetic

To **add two negative** numbers, add the 'numbers' and make the answer negative.

Example
$-4 + -3$ or $-4 - 3 = -7$

To **add a negative and a positive** number, take the smaller away from the bigger and give it the sign of the 'bigger number'

Examples
$-11 + 4 = -(11 - 4) = -7$
$5 + -7$ or $5 - 7 = -(7 - 5) = -2$

To **subtract a negative** number, you read the two minuses $- -$ as a $+$

Example
$5 - -3 = 5 + 3 = 8$

The rules for **multiplying and dividing with negative** numbers are very easy after you have learnt the addition and subtraction:

> ▶ If the signs are the same, the answer is a positive.
> ▶ If the signs are different, the answer is a negative.

Examples
$2 \times 5 = 10$, $-3 \times -4 = 12$, $15 \div -3 = -5$, $-18 \div -3 = 6$

Decimal number
Change a fraction to a decimal by dividing the top by the bottom.

Example
Change $\frac{5}{8}$ to a decimal number. Divide 5 by 8 to give 0.625

Decimal places
When a number is written in decimal form, the digits on the right-hand side of the decimal point are called the decimal places.

Example
83.7 is written to one decimal place (1 d.p.).
0.439 is written to three decimal places (3 d.p.).

Rules to round a decimal number off to a particular number of places are:

> ▶ count the particular number of decimal places from the decimal point and look at the first digit you are going to remove
> ▶ if this digit is less than 5 then just remove the unwanted places
> ▶ if this digit is 5 or more, then add 1 onto the last decimal place digit

Examples
4.751 will round off to 4.75 to two decimal places
0.382 will round off to 0.4 to one decimal place
23.6526 will round off to 23.7 to one decimal place

Significant figures
We often use significant figures when we want to approximate a number with quite a few digits in it. The number of significant figures to which a number is written is the number of 'real' (non-zero) digits which appear together in a number.

Example
Look at this table of various numbers of significant figures (s.f.)

One s.f.	7	40	300	80 000	0.00004	0.002
Two s.f.	84	9.3	0.47	21 000	390	0.0053

Note that when the zeros come at the end of the number or at the beginning, we do not count them. However when the zeros come between digits, we *do* count them. So 405 has 3 significant figures.

Rules to round a number off to a particular number of significant figures are very similar to the rules for decimal places:

> ▶ from the left, count the particular number of digits of the given significant figure
> ▶ look at the next digit
> ▶ if this is less than 5 , then leave the digits on the left the same
> ▶ if this digit is 5 or more then add 1 to the last digit on the left
> ▶ put in enough zeros to keep the number the right size

Examples
836 to 2 s.f. is 840
836 to 1 s.f. is 800

Approximation

Example
Approximately, what is the answer to 26.3×7.48?
To approximate the answer to this and to many other similar situations we simply round each number off to 1 s.f. then work it out.
So the approximation of our sum will be

$$26.3 \times 7.48 \approx 30 \times 7 = 210$$

Sometimes, especially when dividing, we round a number off to something useful at 2 s.f. instead of the 1 s.f. number.

Example
Approximately, what is the answer to $49.2 \div 6.37$? Since the 6.37 rounds off to 6, then let's round the 49.2 off to 48 since 6 divides exactly into 48. Hence

$$49.2 \div 6.37 \approx 48 \div 6 = 8$$

A quick approximation is always a good help in any calculation since it often stops you writing down a silly answer.

Percentage
You should know that to find $A\%$ of an amount P, you calculate $(A \times P) \div 100$.

Example
7% of 40 kg is

$$(7 \times 40) \div 100 = 2.8 \, \text{kg}$$

You should know that any percentage can be represented as a decimal by dividing by 100.

Example
$$65\% = 65 \div 100 = 0.65$$

You should know the common fractions expressed as a percentage.

Example
$$\frac{1}{2} = 50\% \quad \frac{1}{4} = 25\% \quad \frac{3}{4} = 75\% \quad \frac{1}{10} = 10\% \quad \frac{1}{5} = 20\% \quad \frac{1}{3} = 33\frac{1}{3}\%$$

> ▶ **Percentage increase**
> Change the percentage to a decimal , add 1 , then multiply by the figure that needs increasing.

Example
Increase £6 by 5%. Change 5% to decimal, add 1, then multiply by £6. Hence

$$1.05 \times £6 = £6.30$$

▶ **Percentage decrease**
Change the percentage to a decimal and take it away from 1, then multiply it by the original figure.

Example
Decrease £8 by 4%. Change 4% to a decimal and take it away from 1.

$1 - 0.04 = 0.96$

Multiply this by the original

$0.96 \times £8 = £7.68$

▶ **'As a percentage'**
We express one quantity as a percentage of another by setting up the two numbers as a fraction of each other and converting that fraction to a percentage by simply multiplying by 100.

Example
Express £7 as a percentage of £25.

Set up the fraction $\frac{7}{25}$ and multiply by 100. This becomes

$(7 \div 25) \times 100 = 28\%$

▶ **Reverse percentage**
There are times when we know a certain percentage and we wish to get back to the original amount.

Example
The 31 pupils who were absent represented only 4% of the pupils in the school. How many pupils should have been at school?

Since 4% represents 31 pupils, then 1% will represent $31 \div 4$ pupils $= 7.75$, so 100% will be represented by

$(7.75 \times 100) = 775$ pupils

Ratios
To divide any amount in a given ratio, you simply multiply the amount by the fraction of the ratio.

Example
Divide £60 between John and Kevin in the ratio of 2 : 3.

From the ratio we see that John receives $\frac{2}{5}$ and Kevin receives $\frac{3}{5}$. Hence

John receives $£60 \times \frac{2}{5} = £24$ and

Kevin receives $£60 \times \frac{3}{5} = £36$

Sometimes you may know only part of the information.

Example
Two business partners Sue and Trish divide their profits in the ratio 3 : 5. If Sue receives £1 800 how much does Trish receive?

Sue receives £1 800 which is $\frac{3}{8}$ of the whole profit. So $\frac{1}{8} = £1\,800 \div 3 = £600$. So Trish's share which is $\frac{5}{8}$ will be

$£600 \times 5 = £3\,000$

Speed

The connection between speed , time and distance is

$$\text{Speed} = \frac{\text{Distance}}{\text{Time}}; \quad \text{Distance} = \text{Speed} \times \text{Time}; \quad \text{Time} = \frac{\text{Distance}}{\text{Speed}}$$

When we refer to speed we usually mean average speed , as it is unusual to maintain one exact speed for the whole of one journey.

Prime factors

Finding prime factors involves splitting a number up into factors that are all prime.

Examples
$110 = 2 \times 5 \times 11$
$24 = 2 \times 2 \times 2 \times 3$

A quicker and neater way to write this answer is using *index notation*.
Prime factors of $24 = 2^3 \times 3$

Special numbers

Some special numbers with which you should be familiar are:

▶ Square numbers   1, 4, 9, 16, 25, ...
▶ Prime numbers   2, 3, 5, 7, 11, 13, ...
▶ Multiples of A are numbers that will divide exactly by A
▶ Factors of B are numbers that will divide exactly into B

Standard form

This is writing large and small numbers using powers of 10. The definition is
$a \times 10^n$ where $1 < a < 10$, and n is a whole number.

Examples
$$82.1 = 8.21 \times 10 = 8.21 \times 10^1$$
$$325 = 3.25 \times 100 = 3.25 \times 10^2$$
$$4728 = 4.728 \times 1\,000 = 4.728 \times 10^3$$
$$0.0034 = 3.4 \div 1\,000 = 3.4 \times 10^{-3}$$

REVISION ACTIVITY

Complete the following.

1 Write down the first eight, (a) prime numbers, (b) square numbers.
2 What are the prime factors of (a) 144, (ii) 140?
3 Without a calculator, calculate (a) 257×35, (b) $741 \div 13$.
4 (a) Increase 5 kg by 17%. (b) Decrease 5 m by 21%.
5 A baby octopus increases its weight by 5% every day of its young life. What is the weight of a 5-day-old baby octopus which was born at 8.5 kg?
6 Convert the following numbers into standard form.
   (a) 9684   (b) 50 000   (c) 38 200
   (d) 0.0095   (e) 8 million   (f) 0.867
7 Without using a calculator, estimate what value the following have.
   (a) 36.8×21.6 (b) $562 \div 6.7$ (c) $\dfrac{134 \times 57.3}{7.5}$ (d) $8.3^2 + 9.7^2$

8 Correct each of the following to the number of decimal places or significant figures indicated.
  (a) 2.643 (2 d.p.)   (b) 1.338 (2 d.p.)   (c) 17.64 (1 d.p.)
  (d) 7.5474 (2 s.f.)   (e) 17.6 (1 s.f.)   (f) 0.00587 (1 s.f.)

9 Divide £325 in the ratio 2 : 3.

10 Express each of the following as a percentage.
  (a) £5 out of £24
  (b) 4 kg out of 32 kg
  (c) 2.5 m out of 10 m

PRACTICE QUESTIONS

1 Do not use a calculator when answering this question. All working must be shown.
  A man wants to put his 600 programmes into boxes. Each box can store 44 programmes. How many boxes can he fill and how many programmes will be left over?

  ....
  ....
  ....
  ....

2 Do not use a calculator when answering this question. All working must be shown.

  Obtain an **estimate** for $\dfrac{674 \times 89}{38}$.

  ....
  ....
  ....

3 The size of the crowd at a football match is given as 27 800 to the nearest hundred.
  (a) What is the lowest number that the crowd could be?

  ....

  (b) What is the largest number that the crowd could be?

  ....

4 Margaret earned £270 each week. She gets a pay increase of 4%. How much is her weekly pay now?

  ....
  ....
  ....

5 List the following in size, starting with the smallest.
  $\frac{3}{8}$, 0.4, 0.23, 39%

  ....

6 Sarah invests £120 in a bank account at an interest rate of 7.8% per annum.
(a) Calculate the interest on £120 after 1 year.

....

....

....

At the end of the each year the interest is added to her bank account.
(b) Calculate the total amount of money in Sarah's bank account if she keeps all her money in for 3 years.

....

....

....

....

7 Televisions were advertised at: Normal price £435   Sale price £295
Find the percentage reduction on the televisions in the sale.

....

....

....

8 Three strikers score 21,15 and 9 goals respectively. Their club pays out £9 000 in bonus money to these players. They share the bonus in the same ratio as the goals they score. Calculate the share of the bonus for each player.

....

....

....

9 Write down:
(a) a square number bigger than 20

....

(b) a factor of 100 bigger than 30

....

(c) a multiple of 5 bigger than 40

....

(d) a prime number bigger than 50

....

10 A light year is the distance travelled by light in 365 days. The speed of light is 3.0×10^5 kilometres per second. The distance to the star system Krul is 7.0×10^{23} kilometres.
How many light years is it to the system Krul? Give your answer to an appropriate degree of accuracy.

....

....

....

Algebra

You need to be familiar with the processes of algebra.

Substitution

One of the most important features of algebra is the use of expressions and formulae and the substitution of real numbers into them.

The value of an *expression* such as $3x + 2$ will change with the different values of x substituted into it.

Example
The expression $3x + 2$ will be 5 when $x = 1$

Similarly a *formula* can be used to evaluate one variable as others change.

Example
The formula for the area of a trapezium is given by $A = \dfrac{h(a + b)}{2}$.
If $a = 4$, $b = 7$ and $h = 8$ then

$$A = \frac{8(4 + 7)}{2} = 44$$

Solving equations

The first type of equation we need to be able to solve is the **linear equation**.

Example
Solve $5(2x - 9) = 14$.

If we multiply out the brackets first, we get

$$10x - 45 = 14$$

We can move the 45 to give $\quad 10x = 14 + 45 = 59$
We can move the 10 to give $\quad x = \frac{59}{10}$
$$x = 5.9$$

Trial and improvement

Example
Solve the equation $x^2 + x = 80$ giving your solution to 2 decimal places.

▶ We must first find the two whole numbers that x lies between. We do this by intelligent guessing.
Try $x = 9$: $\quad 81 + 9 = 90 \quad$ too high, so next trial needs to be smaller
Try $x = 8$: $\quad 64 + 8 = 72 \quad$ too low
but we now know that the solution is between 8 and 9.
▶ We must now try halfway between 8 and 9 which is 8.5
Try 8.5: $\quad 72.25 + 8.5 = 80.75 \quad$ too large,
▶ We can see, though, that we are very close so we can improve the trial by trying 8.4.
Try 8.4: $\quad 70.56 + 8.4 = 78.96 \quad$ too low

▶ We now have to try halfway between 8.4 and 8.5 which is 8.45
   Try 8.45: $71.4025 + 8.45 = 79.8525$ too low
▶ We are too low, so try between 8.45 and 8.5 (close to halfway)
   Try 8.47: $71.7409 + 8.47 = 80.2109$ too high
   Try 8.46: $71.5716 + 8.46 = 80.0316$ too high
▶ We now know that the solution is between 8.45 and 8.46 but which is closer?
   To find which is closer we cannot just look at the numbers we have because
   the differences do not go up uniformly. We have to try halfway between them
   again and go from there. Halfway between 8.45 and 8.46 is 8.455
   Try 8.455: $71.487025 + 8.455 = 79.942025$ too low
   The solution is nearest to 8.46 (2 d.p.)

Simultaneous equations

Example 1
Solve the simultaneous equations $6x + y = 15$
$$4x + y = 11$$

Since both equations have a y term of the same magnitude we can *subtract*
one equation from the other to give

$$2x = 4$$
which solves to give $x = 2$

We now substitute $x = 2$ into one of the initial equations (usually the one
with the smallest numbers involved). So substitute into $4x + y = 11$ to give

$$8 + y = 11$$
which gives $y = 11 - 8$
$$y = 3$$

We test our solution in the other initial equation.
Substitute $x = 2$ and $y = 3$ into $6x + y$ to give $12 + 3 = 15$, which is
correct. So we can confidently say that our solution is $x = 2$ and $y = 3$.

Example 2
Solve the simultaneous equations $4x - 2y = 12$
$$2x + 2y = 18$$

Since both equations have a $2y$ term but one with a $+$ and one with a $-$, then
we can *add* one equation to the other to give

$6x = 30$
$x = 5$

Substitute $x = 5$ into, say, the second equation to get

$2 \times 5 + 2y = 18$
   $10 + 2y = 18$
      $2y = 18 - 10 = 8$
      $y = 4$

The solution of $x = 5$ and $y = 4$ can be checked in the top equation to give

$(4 \times 5) - (2 \times 4) = 20 - 8 = 12$

which is correct. So our solution is $x = 5$ and $y = 4$.

Example 3
Solve the simultaneous equations $4x + 2y = 32$
$$3x - y = 19$$

Here we do not have any equal terms so we have to start creating them because that is the only way we can solve simultaneous equations. We can see that by multiplying *all* of the second equation by 2 we get

$$(3x - y = 19) \times 2 \quad \Rightarrow \quad 6x - 2y = 38$$

Our pair of equations is now $\quad 4x + 2y = 32$
$$6x - 2y = 38$$

and we can solve these like we did in Example 2.

Example 4
Solve the simultaneous equations $\quad 5x + 4y = 22$
$$2x + 3y = 6$$

Notice we cannot simply multiply one equation by anything to give us some equal terms. So we have to multiply *both* equations by appropriate numbers.

The choice is now up to us, we can either make the xs the same or the ys the same. Sometimes there is an obvious choice; sometimes it doesn't matter. In this example it doesn't matter which you do since there is no great advantage in choosing either.

Lets choose xs to be made equal. We will have to multiply the first equation through by 2 and the second equation through by 5. This gives

$$(5x + 4y = 22) \times 2 \quad \Rightarrow \quad 10x + 8y = 44$$
$$(2x + 3y = 6) \times 5 \quad \Rightarrow \quad 10x + 15y = 30$$

We now solve these in the same way as we did in Example 1.

Problems solved by simultaneous equations

Suppose we are given a problem that looks like simultaneous equations, for example, 'Two teas and five buns cost £1.04 and three teas and two buns cost £1.01. How much is tea and a bun?' We simply replace the words 'tea' and 'bun' with t and b so the equations to solve become

$$2t + 5b = 104$$
$$3t + 2b = 101$$

and we solve as before.

Inequalities

Inequalities behave similarly to normal equations. The difference is that they have an inequality sign instead of an equality one.

For linear inequalities we use the same rules to solve inequalities as we do linear equations.

Example 1

Solve $\dfrac{5x + 7}{3} < 14$

$$5x + 7 < 14 \times 3$$
$$5x + 7 < 42$$
$$5x < 42 - 7$$
$$5x < 35$$
$$x < 35 \div 5$$
$$x < 7$$

Example 2
Solve the inequality $1 < 5x + 3 \leqslant 17$.

We need to treat each side separately as

$$
\begin{array}{ll}
1 < 5x + 3 & 5x + 3 \leqslant 17 \\
1 - 3 < 5x & 5x \leqslant 17 - 3 \\
-2 < 5x & 5x \leqslant 14 \\
\dfrac{-2}{5} < x & x \leqslant \dfrac{14}{5} \\
-0.4 < x & x \leqslant 2.8
\end{array}
$$

Hence $-0.4 < x \leqslant 2.8$

Inequalities involving x^2

Consider $x^2 < 16$. The solution to $x^2 = 16$ is $x = 4$ and $x = -4$. When we look at the $x = 4$ part we can see that, yes, $x < 4$ fits the solution to the original inequality, but for the $x = -4$ part we can see that $x < -4$ just does not work. In fact the solution to do with $x = -4$ needs the inequality sign changing round to give us the solution $x > -4$ which can be turned to give $-4 < x$. Put all this onto a number line and you see the solution.

The solution is $-4 < x < 4$.

Indices

You should be familiar with indices.

Examples

$$
\begin{array}{ll}
m \times m = m^2 & \\
4m \times 2m = 8m^2 & \\
3m^2 \times 5m = 15m^3 & \text{remember, we add the indices } (5m = 5m^1) \\
3m^3 \times 2m^2 = 6m^5 & \text{remember to add the indices } 3 + 2 = 5 \\
m^5 \div m^3 = m^2 & \text{remember to subtract the indices} \\
8m^7 \div 2m^6 = 4m &
\end{array}
$$

Expansion

This is the multiplication of terms in one or more brackets. The examples below involve a single bracket.

Examples

$$
\begin{array}{ll}
2(3t + 4) = 6t + 8 & p(p^2 - 5x) = p^3 - 5px \\
k(p + 6) = kp + 6k & 4x^2(2x + 7) = 8x^3 + 28x^2 \\
3t(t + 5) = 3t^2 + 15t & -3t(2 - 4t) = -6t + 12t^2
\end{array}
$$

Simplification

Examples

$$3(5 + p) + 2(4 + 3p) = 15 + 3p + 8 + 6p$$
$$= 23 + 9p$$
$$3w(4w + 1) - w(3w - 7) = 12w^2 + 3w - 3w^2 + 7w$$
$$= 9w^2 + 10w$$

Quadratic expansion

When we have an expression such as $(5y + 2)(2y - 3)$ then it can be expanded and a quadratic expression can clearly be seen.

It is the *multiplying out* of such pairs of brackets that is usually called a quadratic expansion.

The rule for expanding such expressions as $(x + 4)(3x - 3)$ is similar to expanding single brackets: multiply everything in one bracket with everything in the other bracket.

Example 1

$$(x + 2)(x + 3) = x(x + 3) + 2(x + 3)$$
$$= x^2 + 3x + 2x + 6$$
$$= x^2 + 5x + 6$$

Example 2

$$(y + 6)(y - 3) = y(y - 3) + 6(y - 3)$$
$$= y^2 - 3y + 6y - 18$$
$$= y^2 + 3y - 18$$

Example 3

$$(t - 2)(t + 1) = t(t + 1) - 2(t + 1)$$
$$= t^2 + t - 2t - 2$$
$$= t^2 - t - 2$$

Example 4

$$(q - 4)(q - 2) = q(q - 2) - 4(q - 2)$$
$$= q^2 - 2q - 4q + 8$$
$$= q^2 - 6q + 8$$

Example 5

$$(3t + 2)(2t - 1) = 3t(2t - 1) + 2(2t - 1)$$
$$= 6t^2 - 3t + 4t - 2$$
$$= 6t^2 + t - 2$$

Expanding squares

Example

$$(2x - 5)^2 = (2x - 5)(2x - 5) = 2x(2x - 5) - 5(2x - 5)$$
$$= 4x^2 - 10x - 10x + 25$$
$$= 4x^2 - 20x + 25$$

Factorisation

This involves re-arranging an expression into one or more brackets.

Examples

$$4t + 6m = 2(2t + 3m) \qquad\qquad 5p^2 - 25p = 5p(p - 5)$$
$$6mt + 9pt = 3t(2m + 3p) \qquad 12px + 4tx - 8mx = 4x(3p + t - 2m)$$

Quadratic factorisation

This involves re-arranging an expression involving x^2 into two brackets multiplied together.

Example 1

Factorise $x^2 + 9x + 20$.

We note that both brackets start with an x: $(x\ \ )(x\ \ )$.
We see that the second sign is positive, hence both bracket signs will be the same as the first sign, which is plus: $(x +\ \ )(x +\ \ )$.
We note that the second numbers in each bracket must multiply together to give 20, i.e. (1, 20) or (2, 10) or (4, 5).
We note that the signs in the brackets are the same, so these numbers add up to 9. Hence this must be the (4, 5) choice.
Hence the factorisation is $(x + 4)(x + 5)$.

Example 2

Factorise $x^2 - 7x + 10$.

We note that both brackets start with an x: $(x\ \ )(x\ \ )$.
We see that the second sign is positive, so both bracket signs will be the same as the first sign, which is minus: $(x -\ \ )(x -\ \ )$.
We note that the second numbers in each bracket must multiply together to give 10, i.e. (1, 10) or (2, 5).
We note that the signs in the brackets are the same, so these numbers add up to 7. Hence this must be the (2, 5) choice.
Hence the factorisation is $(x - 2)(x - 5)$.

Difference of two squares

Example

Factorise $x^2 - n^2$.

This factorises to $(x + n)(x - n)$.

Solving quadratic equations as $x^2 + ax + b = 0$

Example 1

Solve $x^2 + 2x - 15 = 0$.

This factorises into $(x - 3)(x + 5) = 0$.
The only way that this expression can ever equal 0 is if one of the brackets is worth 0. Hence either

$$(x - 3) = 0 \quad \text{or} \quad (x + 5) = 0$$

hence $\qquad\quad x - 3 = 0 \quad \text{or} \qquad x + 5 = 0$

hence $\qquad\qquad\quad x = 3 \quad \text{or} \qquad\quad x = -5$

The solution then is $x = 3$ and -5.

Transformation of formulae

Example 1

From the formula $T = 4m - 1$, make m the subject.

$T + 1 = 4m$ (moving the 1 away from the $4m$)

$\dfrac{T + 1}{4} = m$ (moving the 4 away from the m)

Hence the transformed formula becomes

$$m = \frac{T + 1}{4}$$

Example 2

From the formula $Q = 7(2t + 3)$, express t in terms of Q.
(This is just another way of asking you to make t the subject.)

$Q = 14t + 21$ (expanding the bracket)

$Q - 21 = 14t$ (moving the 21 away from the $14t$)

$\dfrac{Q - 21}{14} = t$ (moving the 14 away from the t)

Hence the transformed formula becomes

$$t = \frac{Q - 21}{14}$$

REVISION ACTIVITY

Complete the following.

1 Solve the following pairs of simultaneous equations.
  (a) $5x + y = 0$ (b) $7x + 3y = 18$
       $3x - 2y = 13$ $x + y = 4$

2 Expand the following and simplify.
  (a) $(4x - 5)(3x - 1)$ (b) $(2x + 3)(3x - 2)$
  (c) $p(2m + t) - t(3m - p)$

3 Solve the following equations.
  (a) $2x + 3 = 12$ (b) $10 - 5x = 3$ (c) $5(2x - 3) = 8$

4 Make y the subject of the following formulae.
  (a) $x = 2(y - 1)$ (b) $x = y(b + 7)$ (c) $t = \dfrac{5y + p}{7}$

5 Solve the following by trial and improvement, to 2 decimal places.
  (a) $x^3 = 100$ (b) $x(x + 5) = 333$ (c) $x^3 + x = 75$

6 Factorise the following.
  (a) $3t + 7t^2$ (b) $2m^3 - 6m^2$ (c) $6mp^3 + 9m^2pt$

7 Factorise the following.
  (a) $x^2 + 5x + 6$ (b) $x^2 - 8x + 15$ (c) $x^2 + 2x - 15$

8 Solve the following quadratic equations.
  (a) $x^2 + 7x + 12 = 0$ (b) $x^2 + x - 6 = 0$

9 Factorise the following.
  (a) $x^2 - 25$ (b) $t^2 - p^2$ (c) $m^2 + 6m + 9$

10 Solve the following inequalities.
  (a) $5x > 32$ (b) $4t < 5t - 8$ (c) $x^2 < 36$
  (d) $-2 \leqslant 5x + 3 < 4$

PRACTICE QUESTIONS

1 Given that $m = 0.5$, $p = 0.75$ and $t = -4$, calculate

(a) $mp + t$

....

....

....

(b) $\dfrac{(m + p)}{t}$

....

....

....

2 Solve the following equations.

(a) $7x = 42$

....

(b) $5t + 6 = 14$

....

....

(c) $3x + 6 = 20 - x$

....

....

3 Cans of pop cost 35 pence each. Write down a formula for the cost, C pence, of n cans of pop.

....

4 Edward sold 30 tickets for a concert. He sold x tickets at £3 each and y tickets at £4.50 each. He collected £123.

(a) Write down two equations connecting x and y.

....

....

(b) Solve these simultaneous equations to find how many of each kind of ticket he sold.

....

....

....

....

....

....

5 (a) Solve the inequality $5n - 8 > 22 + n$

....
....
....

(b) Write down the least whole number value of n that satisfies this inequality.

....

6 Solve the inequality $x^2 < 81$

....
....
....
....

7 The price, £P, of a cruise lasting t days is represented by the formula

$P = 40t + t^2$

(a) What is the price of a cruise lasting 5 days?

....
....
....

(b) The cost, £C, to run the cruise for t days is represented by the formula

$C = 500 + 80t$

(i) Rearrange this formula to make t the subject.

....
....

(ii) The cost of running a cruise was £900. For how many days did this cruise last?

....
....

8 Factorise fully $3t + 6t^2$.

....
....

9 (a) Expand $(3x + 2)(x - 4)$.

....
....
....

(b) Factorise completely $6t^2 - 9t$.

....
....

10 A rectangle has a length of $(x + 5)$ cm and a width of $(x - 2)$ cm.

(a) If the perimeter of the rectangle is 24 cm, what is the value of x?

....

....

(b) If the area of the rectangle is 60 cm^2, show that $x^2 + 3x - 70 = 0$.

....

....

....

(c) Find the value of x when the area of the rectangle is 60 cm^2.

....

....

....

....

11 This is an approximate rule to change a temperature in degrees Celsius (C), into one in degrees Fahrenheit (F).

> Double the Celsius temperature then add 30.

(a) Write this approximate rule as a formula for F in terms of C.

....

....

(b) Use your formula, or otherwise, to find

(i) F when C = 68

....

....

(ii) C when F = 68

....

....

Graphs

TOPIC OUTLINE AND REVISION TIPS

Features of graphs

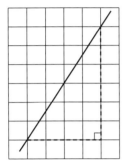

Fig. 1

Gradients

The gradient of a straight line is a measure of its slope.

The gradient of the line shown in Fig. 1 can be measured by drawing a right-angled triangle (as big as possible) having the line as the hypotenuse (sloping side).
The gradient is then found by the following rule

$$\text{Gradient} = \frac{\text{Distance measured up}}{\text{Distance measured along}}$$

Change of units

To change a quantity in one set of units to another set of units, you need to change the units stage by stage. This example will remind you of the process.

Example
Change 18 metres per second to kilometres per hour.

18 m/s = 18 × 60 × 60 metres per hour = 64 800 m/h
64 800 m/h = 64 800 ÷ 1 000 km/h = 64.8 km/h

Types of graph

Conversion graphs

Figure 2 illustrates the charge for gas in 1996.

Fig. 2

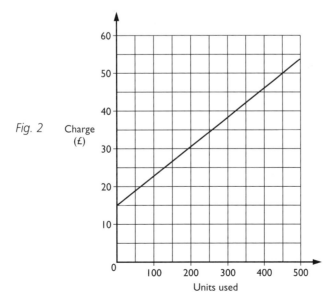

Charge (£) / Units used

We can see from the graph that:

▶ if a customer uses 400 units of gas he will be charged about £46;

▶ if you received a bill for £30 then you will have used around 190 units.

You need to be able to read these types of graphs by finding one value on one axis and following it through to the value on the other axis as shown above.

Travel graphs

As the name suggests, travel graphs give information about how something has travelled. They are also called *distance/time graphs*.

You can find information from a travel graph by reading the graph in the same way as you did with Fig. 2.

You can also find the average speed, from a distance/time graph by using the simple formula

$$\text{Average speed} = \frac{\text{Total distance travelled}}{\text{Total time}}$$

Example

The distance/time graph in Fig. 3 represents a car journey from Sheffield to Cambridge, a distance of 120 miles, and back again.

Fig. 3

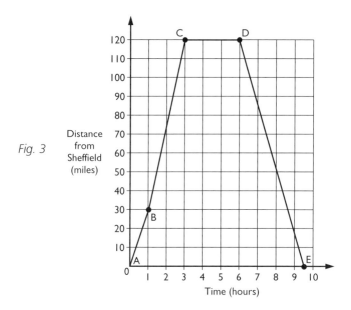

We can read that:

▶ after 1 hour the car was 30 miles away from Sheffield;

▶ after 3 hours the car was 120 miles away from Sheffield and at Cambridge;

▶ the car stayed at Cambridge for 3 hours;

▶ the return journey took $3\frac{1}{2}$ hours.

We can work out the average speeds as follows.

▶ A to B on the graph represents 30 miles in 1 hour, which is 30 mph.

▶ B to C represents 90 miles in 2 hours. Dividing both numbers by 2 gives us 45 miles in 1 hour, which is 45 mph.

▶ C to D represents a stop, where no more distance has been travelled.

▶ D to E represents the return journey of 120 miles in $3\frac{1}{2}$ hours. Divide 120 by 3.5 to give miles per hour: $120 \div 3.5 = 34.3$. Hence the return journey was at an average speed of 34.3 mph.

Graphs from equations

If you have an equation connecting two variables then you can draw a graph to represent it. There are different types of equation which give different types and shapes of graph.

► **Graphs from linear equations**

Graphs from linear equations will always be straight lines. You need only three points to be sure of your line.

Example

Draw the graph of $y = 2x + 3$.

Choose different values of x and see what the corresponding value of y is when you substitute the value for x into $y = 2x + 3$.

x	0	2	4
y	3	7	11

Plot these points on a grid and join up the points. You should have a straight line.

Every linear equation can be written in the form

$$y = mx + c$$

If this is then graphed you will always find that m = the gradient of the line and c = the place where the line cuts the y-axis.

   If a graph can be expressed in the form $y = mx + c$ then the value *in front of x* is the *gradient*. We call this value m. The *constant* term gives the *intercept* on the y-axis. We call this value c.

   This means that if we know the gradient, m, of a line, say 5, and we know the intercept, c, of the line with the y-axis, say -2, we can write down the equation of the line immediately: in this case $y = 5x - 2$.

   This gives us a method of finding the equation of any line drawn on a pair of coordinate axes.

Example

Find the equation of the line shown in Fig. 4.

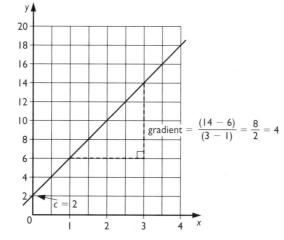

Fig. 4

First we look at the graph to find out where it crosses the y-axis: $c = 2$. Secondly we measure the gradient of the line (see the diagram): $m = 4$. Thirdly write down the equation of the line: $y = 4x + 2$.

Another special type of straight line is one given by an equation of the form

$$ax + by = c$$

This type of equation can be drawn very easily without much working at all. The following is an example of the 'cover and draw' method.

Example
Draw the graph of the equation $4x + 3y = 18$.

Look at the working in Fig. 5 to see how we use the 'cover and draw' method.

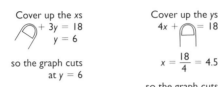

Cover up the xs
$ + 3y = 18$
$y = 6$

so the graph cuts
at $y = 6$

Cover up the ys
$4x + = 18$

$x = \dfrac{18}{4} = 4.5$

so the graph cuts
at $x = 4.5$

Fig. 5

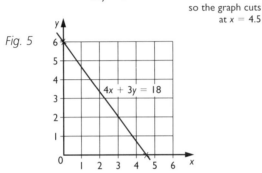

▶ **Graphs from quadratic equations**
A quadratic equation can always be written in the form

$$y = ax^2 + bx + c$$

The c is just like the linear equation, it tells where the curve cuts the y-axis.

Any graph from a quadratic equation will look like Fig. 6.

Fig. 6 $\bigcup$ or $\bigcap$

$a > 0$ $a < 0$

Because it is curved you will need quite a few points in order to plot its shape accurately. You will always be given a table of values or at least the range of x values to choose in order to find the points to plot.
    Two important points to remember when drawing quadratic graphs are:

▶ draw smooth curves;
▶ the curves must have a rounded bottom

Example
Complete the points in the table below then plot the points on the grid and draw the graph of $y = x^2 + 3x - 1$.

The completed table is:

x	-4	-3	-2	-1	0	1	2
x^2	16	9	4	1	0	1	4
$3x$	-12	-9	-6	-3	0	3	6
-1	-1	-1	-1	-1	-1	-1	-1
y	3	-1	-3	-3	-1	3	9

The graph is shown in Fig. 7.

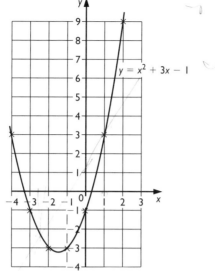

Fig. 7

▶ **Graphs from reciprocal equations**
A reciprocal equation is of the form

$$y = \frac{A}{x}$$

The shape is always like that shown in Fig. 8.

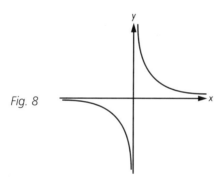

Fig. 8

When $x = 0$ and where $y = 0$ it is impossible to find values for y and x respectively in order to plot. For example, the closer x gets to 0 the larger A/x becomes.

Because of its complex shape you would usually be given a table of values to use to draw the graph.

Solving simultaneous equations graphically

Example
By drawing the graphs find the solution of the simultaneous equations
$4x + y = 8$
$y = 3x - 2$

The first graph is drawn using the 'cover and draw' method. It crosses the *x*-axis at $(2, 0)$ and the *y*-axis at $(0, 8)$.

The second graph can be drawn by finding some points, say $(0, -2)$, $(1, 1)$ and $(3, 7)$.

Putting all this together gives the graphs shown in Fig. 9.

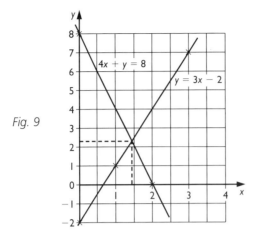

Fig. 9

We can see from the diagram that the point where the graphs intersect is (1.4, 2.3). Hence the solution to the simultaneous equations is $x = 1.4$, $y = 2.3$

Finding regions of graphical inequalities

A two-dimensional inequality is a region that will be on one side or the other of a line. You will recognise it by the fact that it looks like an equation but instead of the equals sign it has an inequality sign, i.e. $<$, $>$, $\leqslant$, or $\geqslant$.
   Each of these means:

$<$ less than
$>$ greater than
$\leqslant$ less than or equal to
$\geqslant$ greater than or equal to

The method for drawing an inequality is to draw the 'boundary line' which is found by replacing the inequality with an equals sign.
   After the boundary is drawn, the appropriate side of the line is shaded. This is found by taking any point that is *not* on the boundary and testing if it works for the inequality. If it works then that is the side required. It if does not work, you want the other side.

Example
Show the region $3x + 2y < 12$.

Draw the line $3x + 2y = 12$.
Test a point *not* on the line, say (0, 0). The origin is always a good choice if possible. Is it true that $3(0) + 2(0) < 12$?
The answer is yes, so the origin is in the side of the line that we want. Shade it in (Fig. 10).

Fig. 10

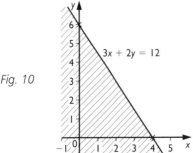

★ REVISION ACTIVITY

Complete the following.

1 The table below shows the results of an experiment on temperature and time.

time (min)	1	2	4	6	8	12	15
temperature (°C)	77	75	69	64	58	48	40

Plot these points on a graph, and use it to find
(a) the time when the temperature was 60°C.
(b) the temperature when the time was 10 minutes.

2 Draw the following graphs.
   (a) $y = 4x - 1$ $(-1 \leqslant x \leqslant 2)$ (b) $3x + 4y = 24$ $(-1 \leqslant x \leqslant 9)$

   (c) $y = x^2 - 1$ $(-3 \leqslant x \leqslant 3)$ (d) $y = \dfrac{12}{x}$ $(-12 \leqslant x \leqslant 12)$

3 Write down an important fact about the graphs of linear equations.
4 Write down the gradient of a straight line joining each of the following pairs of points.
   (a) $(2, 3), (3, 6)$ (b) $(3, 6), (5, 10)$ (c) $(4, 2), (7, 1)$
5 What does the gradient on a distance/time graph tell us?
6 Draw a sketch of the following regions:
   (a) $x > 1$ (b) $y < 5$ (c) $y > x$.

? PRACTICE QUESTIONS

1 Figure 11 is a conversion graph between degrees Celsius, °C, and degrees Fahrenheit, °F.

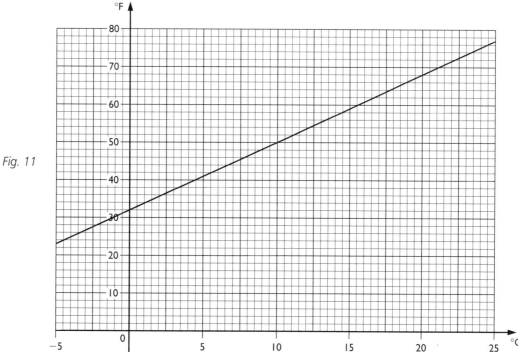

Fig. 11

Use the graph to convert:
(a) 12 °C to degrees Fahrenheit.

....

(b) 75 °F to degrees Celsius.

....

(c) −3 °C to degrees Fahrenheit.

....

2   The distance/time graph in Fig. 12 shows the journeys made by a bus and
a car starting from Cambridge, travelling to Harrow, and returning to
Cambridge.

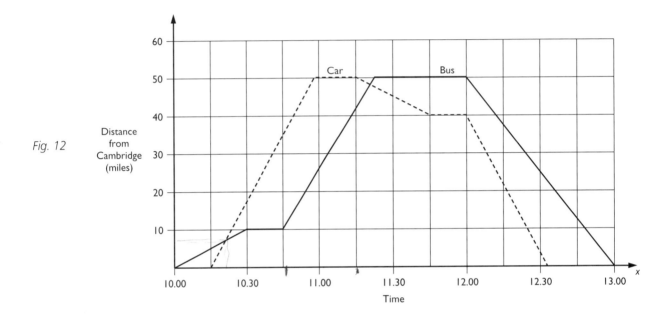

Fig. 12

(a) What time was it and how far had the car travelled when it met the bus
for the first time?

....

(b) Calculate, in miles per hour, the average speed of the bus between 10.45
and 11.15.

....

(c) What was the maximum average speed shown for the car on the graph?

....

3   The table below shows the charge for using different numbers of units of
electricity.

Units	0	200	500	700	900	1000
Charge (£)	15	39	75	99	123	135

(a) Plot these points on a grid.
(b) Use your graph to find
    (i) the charge for using 800 units of electricity.

....

(ii) the charge for using 325 units of electricity.

....

(iii) how many units of electricity have been used if you are charged £80.

....

(c) Explain why the graph does not go through the origin.

....

4 The table below shows the largest quantity of a mineral, m grams, which can be dissolved in a beaker of acid at temperature $t\,°C$.

$t\,°C$	10	20	25	30	40	50	60
m grams	45	49	51	53	57	61	65

(a) On a grid plot the points and draw a graph to illustrate this information.
(b) Use your graph to find the following.
   (i) The lowest temperature at which 54 g of salt will dissolve in water.

....

   (ii) The largest amount of salt that will dissolve in water at 56 °C.

....

(c) The equation of the graph is of the form $m = at + b$. Use your graph to estimate the values of the constants a and b.

....

(d) Use the equation in (c) to calculate the largest amount of salt which will dissolve in the water at 83 °C.

....

....

5 (a) On a pair of axes where $0 \leqslant x \leqslant 6$ and $0 \leqslant y \leqslant 10$ draw the graphs of
   (i) $y = 3x - 2$ and (ii) $y = 5 - x$.
(b) Indicate, on the graph, by suitable shading, the region containing points (x, y) which satisfy all the inequalities $y \geqslant 3x - 2$ and $y \leqslant 5 - x$.

6 Figure 13 is the graph of $y + 5x = 100$. Shade in the region which represents $y + 5x \geqslant 100$.

Fig. 13

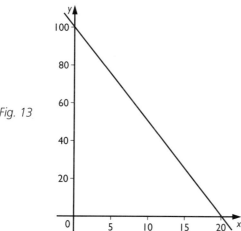

7 Joy buys 2 bags of chips and 4 pieces of fish for £6.
Thomas buys 3 bags of chips and 1 piece of fish for £3.
The cost of 1 bag of chips is £x. The cost of 1 piece of fish is £y.
Therefore $2x + 4y = 6$ and $3x + y = 3$.
(a) Draw the two graphs of these equations.
(b) What is the cost of 1 bag of chips and 1 piece of fish?

....

8 Let $y = x^3 + x$.
(a) Complete the table of values

x	−2	−1	0	1	2
y		−2			

(b) On a grid, where $-2 \leqslant x \leqslant 2$ and $-10 \leqslant y \leqslant 10$, draw the graph of $y = x^3 + x$.
(c) By drawing a suitable straight line on the grid, solve the equation $x^3 + x = 4$.

....

9 (a) Complete the following table of values for $y = \dfrac{6}{x}$, giving your answers to two decimal places where necessary.

x	1	2	3	4	5	6
$y = \dfrac{6}{x}$	6	3				

(b) On a pair of axes, where $0 \leqslant x \leqslant 6$ and $0 \leqslant y \leqslant 6$, draw the graph of $y = \dfrac{6}{x}$.
(c) On the same pair of axes, draw the line AB where A has the coordinates $(1, 1)$ and B has the coordinates $(3, 6)$.
(d) Calculate the gradient of the line AB.

....

(e) Write down the coordinates of the point where the line AB cuts the graph of $y = \dfrac{6}{x}$.

....

Mensuration

TOPIC OUTLINE AND REVISION TIPS

Calculating area

Area of a triangle
The area of a triangle is calculated as

$\frac{1}{2}$ the base length × height

Example
Find the area of the triangle in Fig. 14.

Fig. 14

5 cm

7 cm

Area $= \frac{1}{2} \times 7\,\text{cm} \times 5\,\text{cm} = 17.5\,\text{cm}^2$

Area of a trapezium
The area of a trapezium is found by finding the average of the lengths a and b of the parallel sides and multiplying this by the vertical difference h between them, i.e.

$\text{Area} = h\dfrac{(a+b)}{2}$

Example
Find the area of the trapezium *ABCD* in Fig. 15.

Fig. 15

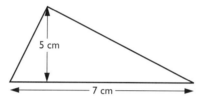

A   3 cm   B

5 cm

D   9 cm   C

Area $= 5 \times \dfrac{(3+9)}{2} = 30\,\text{cm}^2$

Area of a circle
The area of a circle of radius r is given by the rule

$\text{Area} = \pi r^2$

Be careful – this formula uses radius, and if the information you are given is the diameter then you will need to halve the diameter to get your radius.

Example 1
Find the area of a circle with a radius of 6 cm.

Use area $= \pi r^2$

$\pi \times 6^2 = \pi \times 36$ (use π on the calculator)

$= 113\,\text{cm}^2$ (rounded)

Example 2
Find the area of a circle with a diameter of 9 cm.

First halve the diameter to get a radius of 4.5 cm, then use area $= \pi r^2$

$\pi \times 4.5^2 = \pi \times 20.25 = 63.6\,\text{cm}^2$ (rounded)

How to find the circumference of a circle

Circumference $= \pi \times$ Diameter

Do not forget that the value for π is best found by pressing its button on your calculator, but if you have not got access to that button then 3.14 is a good approximation to use.

Example 1
Find the circumference of a circle with a diameter of 6 cm.

Use the formula $C = \pi D$

$\pi \times 6 = 18.8\,\text{cm}$ (rounded)

Example 2
Find the circumference of a circle with a radius of 4.3 cm.

First you need to double the radius to get the diameter, 8.6 cm. Then you can use $C = \pi D$

$\pi \times 8.6 = 27.0\,\text{cm}$ (rounded)

Measuring volume

Volume of a cylinder
The volume of a cylinder is found by multiplying the area of the circular end by the length of the cylinder, i.e.

Volume $= \pi r^2 h$

where r is the radius and h is the height or length.

Example
What is the volume of a cylinder having radius 7 cm and height 15 cm?

Volume = Base area × height

$= \pi r^2 \times h$

$= \pi \times 7^2 \times 15 = 2\,309\,\text{cm}^3$ (rounded)

Volume of a cuboid

The volume of a cuboid is given by

Length × Breadth × Height

Note: Sometimes the height will be referred to as depth.

Example
Find the volume of the cuboid shown in Fig. 16.

Fig. 16

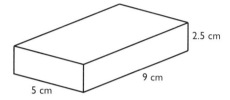

2.5 cm

9 cm

5 cm

$$\begin{aligned} \text{Volume} &= \text{Length} \times \text{Breadth} \times \text{Height} \\ &= 9\,\text{cm} \times 5\,\text{cm} \times 2.5\,\text{cm} \\ &= 112.5\,\text{cm}^3 \end{aligned}$$

Volume of prisms

A prism is a solid shape that has the same cross-section running all the way through it. The volume of a prism is found by multiplying the area of the regular cross-section by its length (or height if stood on end), i.e.

Volume of prism = Area of cross-section × Length

Example
Figure 17 shows a prism with a triangular cross-section. Find the volume of the prism.

Fig. 17

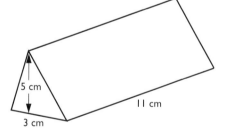

5 cm

11 cm

3 cm

The area of the cross-section is the area of the triangle end, which is

$$\frac{3 \times 5}{2} = 7.5\,\text{cm}^2$$

The volume will be the area of cross-section multiplied by length, which is

$$7.5\,\text{cm}^2 \times 11\,\text{cm} = 82.5\,\text{cm}^3$$

Density

Density is the amount of weight per volume, usually grams per cubic centimetre (g/cm^3). You need to remember that 'weight' is commonly used in Mathematics examination questions, whereas, in science it is always referred to as 'mass'.

The connection between the three is

$$\text{Density} = \frac{\text{Weight}}{\text{Volume}}$$

which can be written as Weight = Density × Volume

Example 1
A piece of metal weighing 25 g has a volume of 8 cm^3. What is its density?

$$\text{Density} = \frac{25}{8} = 3.1 \text{ g/cm}^3 \text{ (rounded)}$$

Example 2
What is the weight of a rock that has a volume of 29 cm^3 and has a density of 1.7 g/cm^3?

Weight = 29 × 1.7 = 49.3 g

REVISION ACTIVITY

Complete the following.

1 Complete the following table for each rectangle (all units are cm or cm^2).

	Length	Breadth	Perimeter	Area
(a)	6	4	......	......
(b)	10	......	30	......
(c)	......	3	......	21

2 Complete the following table for each triangle (all units are cm or cm^2).

	Base	Vertcial height	Area
(a)	6	8	......
(b)	......	3	12
(c)	18	......	27

3 Complete the following table for each trapezium (all units are cm or cm^2).

	Vertical height	Parallel side 1	Parallel side 2	Area
(a)	8	5	6	......
(b)	......	8	4	36
(c)	6	......	11	54

4 Complete the following table for each circle (all units are cm or cm^2).

	Radius	Diameter	Circumference	Area
(a)	7	......	......	......
(b)	......	8.4	......	......
(c)	......	......	22	......
(d)	......	......	......	250

5 Calculate the volumes of the two prisms shown in Fig. 18.

Fig. 18

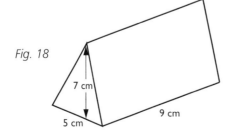

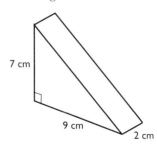

6 Calculate the weight of a solid cuboid with dimensions 10 cm by 6 cm by 3.5 cm and a density of 1.8 g/cm^3.

7 A stone has a volume of 13 cm^3 and weighs 31.5 g. What is its density?

PRACTICE QUESTIONS

1 The radius of the wheel of a bicycle is 28 cm. Calculate the circumference of the wheel.

....

....

2 The radius of a circle is 8 cm. Work out the area of the circle.

....

....

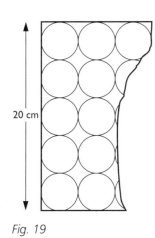

20 cm

Fig. 19

3 Bottle tops are stamped out from rectangular sheets of foil. Each sheet of foil is 60 cm long and 20 cm wide. The diameter of each disc is 4 cm.
Figure 19 shows part of a sheet with discs cut from it.
(a) How many discs can be cut from one sheet of foil?

....

(b) What is the area of one sheet of foil?

....

(c) What is the area of one bottle top?

....

(d) The foil left after the discs are cut out is recycled. What percentage of each sheet of foild is recycled?

....

....

4 Rachel does a sponsored bicycle ride. Each wheel of her bicycle is of radius 25 cm.
(a) Calculate the circumference of one of the wheels.

....

(b) She cycles 50 km. How many revolutions does a wheel make during the sponsored ride?

....

....

5 The floor of a room measures 4.5 m by 5.8 m. The height of the room is 2.8 m. What is the volume of the room?

....

6 A cylinder has a radius of 3.5 cm and a height of 8 cm. Find its volume.

....

....

7 Figure 20 shows a swimming pool. What is the volume of the pool?

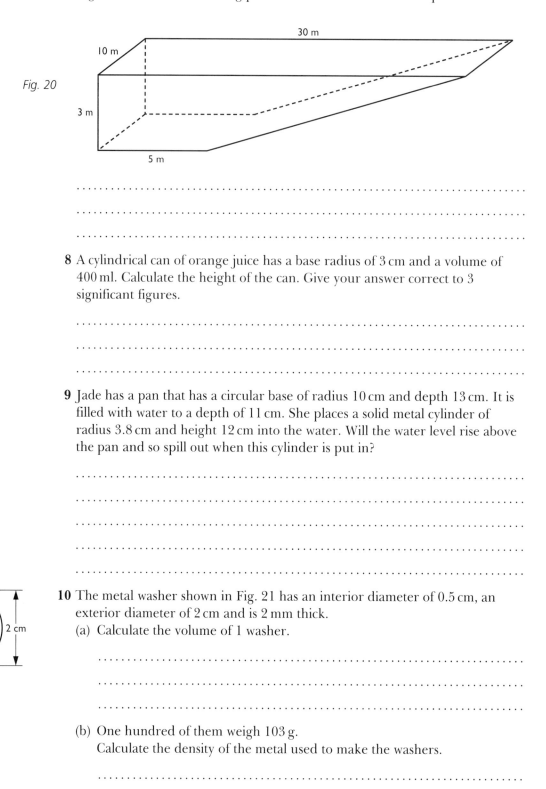

Fig. 20

....

....

....

8 A cylindrical can of orange juice has a base radius of 3 cm and a volume of 400 ml. Calculate the height of the can. Give your answer correct to 3 significant figures.

....

....

....

9 Jade has a pan that has a circular base of radius 10 cm and depth 13 cm. It is filled with water to a depth of 11 cm. She places a solid metal cylinder of radius 3.8 cm and height 12 cm into the water. Will the water level rise above the pan and so spill out when this cylinder is put in?

....

....

....

....

....

10 The metal washer shown in Fig. 21 has an interior diameter of 0.5 cm, an exterior diameter of 2 cm and is 2 mm thick.
   (a) Calculate the volume of 1 washer.

....

....

....

Fig. 21

   (b) One hundred of them weigh 103 g.
       Calculate the density of the metal used to make the washers.

....

....

Similarity and solving triangles

Similar triangles

A pair of triangles are similar if they have the same angles and the corresponding sides are in the same ratio.

Example 1
The triangles *ABC* and *PQR* in Fig. 22 are similar. Find the length of the side *PR*.

Fig. 22

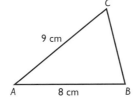 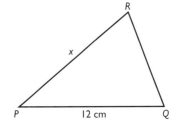

Using pairs of sides that go together, set up an equation using these sides as 'fractions'. These fractions must be equal. The only rule is that the side we are looking for (*x*) must be on the top of one of the fractions, i.e.

$$\frac{PR}{AC} = \frac{PQ}{AB}$$

$$\frac{x}{9} = \frac{12}{8}$$

'Cross-multiply' to find *x*, i.e.

$$x = \frac{9 \times 12}{8} = \frac{108}{8} = 13.5 \text{ cm}$$

Example 2
Find the side *EB* labelled *x* in Fig. 23.

Fig. 23

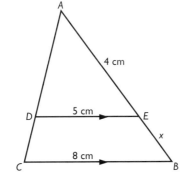

Triangles *AED* and *ABC* are similar. Drawing the two similar triangles out separately (Fig. 24) we can make an equation out of similar sides as

Fig. 24

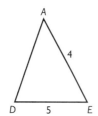 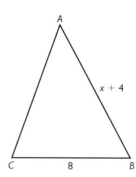

$$\frac{x+4}{4} = \frac{8}{5}$$

$$x + 4 = \frac{8 \times 4}{5} = 6.4$$

so $x = 6.4 - 4 = 2.4\,\text{cm}$

Example 3
Find the side *PT* labelled *x* in Fig. 25.

Fig. 25

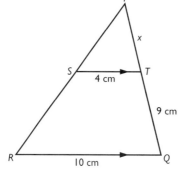

Triangles *PST* and *PRQ* are similar, so drawing them out separately (Fig. 26) gives

Fig. 26

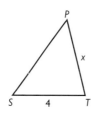 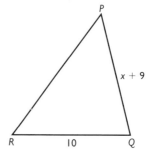

$$\frac{x+9}{x} = \frac{10}{4}$$

Cross-multiplying gives

$$4x + 36 = 10x$$

$$36 = 10x - 4x = 6x$$

$$x = 6\,\text{cm}$$

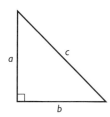

Fig. 27

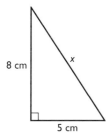

Fig. 28

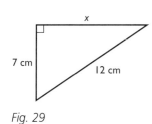

Fig. 29

Pythagoras' theorem

In any right-angled triangle the sum of the squares of the lengths of the two short sides is equal to the square of the hypotenuse.

You will find the rule quoted on the GCSE formula sheet, for the triangle shown in Fig. 27, as

$$a^2 + b^2 = c^2$$

Example 1
Find the length of the hypotenuse in Fig. 28.

$$x^2 = 8^2 + 5^2 = 64 + 25 = 89$$
$$x = \sqrt{89} = 9.4 \text{ cm (rounded)}$$

Example 2
Find the length of the small side x in Fig. 29.

$$x^2 + 7^2 = 12^2$$
$$x^2 = 12^2 - 7^2 = 144 - 49 = 95$$
$$x = \sqrt{95} = 9.7 \text{ cm (rounded)}$$

Trigonometry

We are concerned only with right-angled trigonometry based on a triangle, as in Fig. 30.

Fig. 30

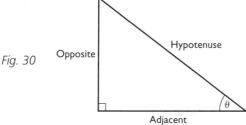

All the relationships are built around these sides as defined by

$$\text{sine } \theta = \frac{\text{opposite}}{\text{hypotenuse}} \qquad \text{cosine } \theta = \frac{\text{adjacent}}{\text{hypotenuse}} \qquad \text{tangent } \theta = \frac{\text{opposite}}{\text{adjacent}}$$

This is best learnt by some mnemonic (saying) such as:

Silly **O**ld **H**itler **C**ouldn't **A**dvance **H**is **T**roops **O**ver **A**frica

which, taking the first letter from each, reminds us that

$$S = \frac{O}{H}, \quad C = \frac{A}{H}, \quad T = \frac{O}{A}.$$

You will find that the full trigonometrical names are usually shortened, as follows:

sine → sin   cosine → cos   tangent → tan

and it is these buttons that you will find on your calculators.

IMPORTANT: Make sure that your calculator is working in degrees. You can usually tell this by a small D or DEG in the display. Depending on the type of calculator you have, you need to be able to put your calculator into degree mode before you start working on sines and cosines. This can be done by

▶ pressing the keys *Mode* then *4*, or by
▶ pressing the key *DRG* until DEG is on display.

Solving problems
If you have a problem to solve that involves trigonometry, it is always best to:

▶ draw a triangle first
▶ put on the given information
▶ then decide which bit of trigonometry you need

Example 1
Find the angle θ given the triangle in Fig. 31.

Fig. 31

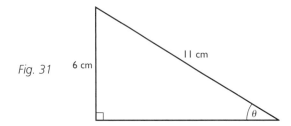

Note the opposite side is 6 cm and that the hypotenuse is 11 cm. We know that opposite and hypotenuse lead us to the sine of the angle

$$\sin \theta = \frac{\text{opposite}}{\text{hypotenuse}} = \frac{6}{11} = 0.545\,454$$

To find the angle, we do not actually need to work out the $0.54\dot{5}\dot{4}$. All we need to do is remember to find the *inverse sin* ($\sin^{-1}$) on the calculator as

| 6 | ÷ | 11 | = | *Shift* | *Sin* |

Warning: There are many different types of calculator around, so get used to the one you will use in the examination. (Your calculator may use 2nd F or something else instead of *Shift*, but whatever it is it is usually the top left hand button on your calculator.)
Check that you were able to get the answer 33.1° (rounded).

Trouble shootout   If you were unable to get the correct answer to the above problem, then check these things;

Wrong answer	Cause	Remedy
0.576 931 3	You are in RAD mode	Put the calculator into DEG mode, either by keying in *Mode 4* or by pressing D/G/R until you get D in the display
36.728 59	You are in GRAD mode	As above
– E –	You probably divided 11 by 6 instead of the correct way round	Divide 6 by 11 first, press = and then access $\sin^{-1}$
56.9 or 28.6	You have used cos or tan instead of using sin	Use the *Sin* key

Example 2
Find the side marked x in the triangle in Fig. 32.

Fig. 32

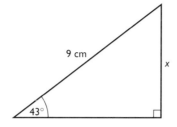

Look to see what kind of side is wanted: it is opposite to the known angle. We are looking for the opposite, with the hypotenuse and an angle known, so use

$$\sin \theta = \frac{\text{opposite}}{\text{hypotenuse}}$$

$$\sin 43° = \frac{\text{opposite}}{9}$$

$$\text{opposite} = 9 \times \sin 43 = 6.1 \text{ cm} \quad \text{(rounded)}$$

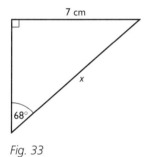

Fig. 33

Example 3
Find the hypotenuse of the triangle in Fig. 33.

We see that we are given the opposite side as 7 cm with the angle known, so use

$$\sin \theta = \frac{\text{opposite}}{\text{hypotenuse}}$$

$$\sin 68° = \frac{7}{\text{hypotenuse}}$$

$$\text{hypotenuse} \times \sin 68° = 7$$

$$\text{hypotenuse} = \frac{7}{\sin 68°} = 7.5 \text{ cm}$$

Example 4
Find the angle θ in the triangle in Fig. 34.

Fig. 34

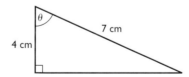

We see that the adjacent side is 4 cm and that the hypotenuse is 7 cm. We use the cosine of the angle.

$$\cos \theta = \frac{\text{adjacent}}{\text{hypotenuse}}$$

$$\cos \theta = \frac{4}{7} = 0.571\,428\,5$$

Use your calculator and $\cos^{-1}$ to find $\theta = 55.2°$ (rounded).

Example 5
Find the side marked *x* in the triangle in Fig. 35.

Fig. 35

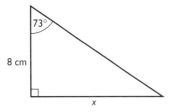

Note that we are looking for the opposite, but the adjacent side and an angle are known, so we use

$$\tan \theta = \frac{\text{opposite}}{\text{adjacent}}$$

$$\tan 73° = \frac{\text{opposite}}{8}$$

$$\text{opposite} = 8 \times \text{tangent } 73°$$
$$= 26.2 \text{ cm (rounded)}$$

Remember that most trigonometry and Pythagoras problems at GCSE do not come in a nice, straightforward triangle. Usually they are part of a realistic problem. In this case, *you must draw a triangle*. Sometimes the triangle is part of the picture that accompanies the problem. Even in this case, *redraw the triangle*. This will avoid any confusion and help you to identify the correct sides and then get the correct ratio.

Example
Jane has a ladder 6 metres long. She leans it against a wall so that the foot of the ladder is 1.5 metres from the wall (Fig. 36). What angle does the ladder make with the wall?

This is a sine problem because we have opposite and hypotenuse.

Fig. 36

$$\sin x = \frac{\text{opposite}}{\text{hypotenuse}}$$

$$\sin x = \frac{1.5}{6} = 0.25$$

$$x = 14.5°$$

REVISION ACTIVITY

Complete the following.

1 Write down the similar triangles for each of the diagrams in Fig. 37.

Fig. 37

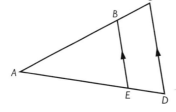
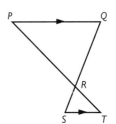

2 Calculate the length marked *x* in each of the diagrams in Fig. 38.

Fig. 38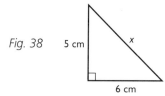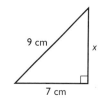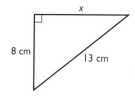

3 In each triangle in Fig. 39, calculate the length *x*.

Fig. 39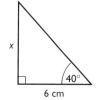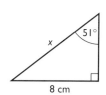

4 In each triangle in Fig. 40, calculate the angle *θ*.

Fig. 40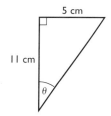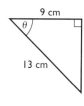

PRACTICE QUESTIONS

1 Calculate the length *ED* in Fig. 41.

Fig. 41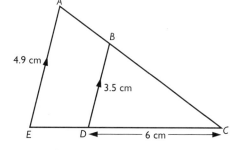

. . . .

. . . .

. . . .

2 I stood about 500 m away from a building. I held a ruler 30 cm long at arm's length, 65 cm away from my eye (Fig. 42). The ruler, held vertically, just blocked the building from my view. Use similar triangles to calculate the height of the building.

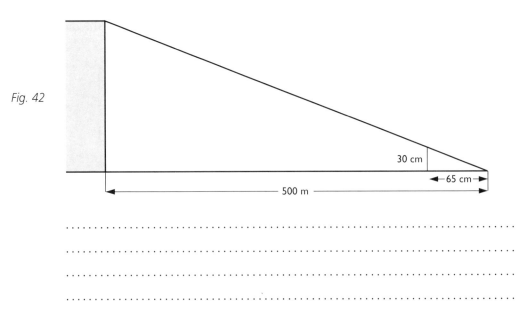

Fig. 42

....

....

....

....

3 Figure 43 shows the end-view of the framework for a building. Calculate the length *AB*.

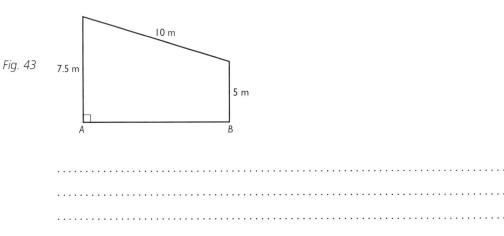

Fig. 43

....

....

....

4

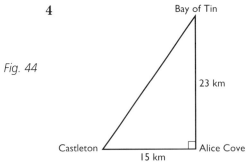

Fig. 44

Figure 44 represents a boat journey from Castleton to Bay of Tin. The boat sails due East from Castleton for 15 km to Alice Cove. The boat then changes course and sails due north for 23 km to Bay of Tin.

On a map, the distance between Castleton and Alice Cove is 12 cm.

(a) Work out the scale of the map.

....

(b) Calculate the distance, in kilometres, from Castleton to Bay of Tin.

....

....

....

5

Fig. 45

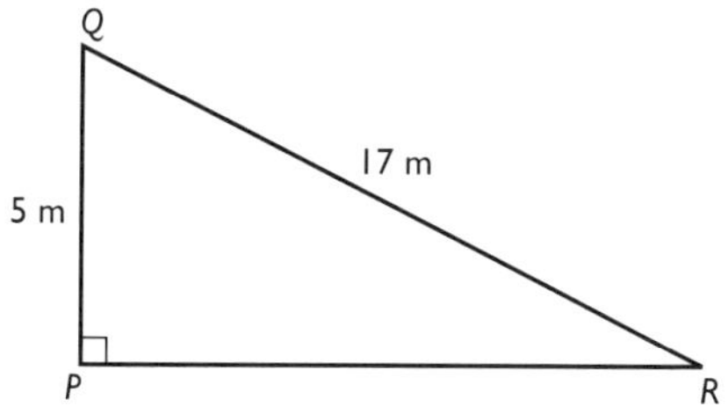

PQR is a right-angled triangle (Fig. 45). *PQ* is of length 5 m and *QR* is of length 17 m. Calculate the length of *PR*.

. . . .

. . . .

. . . .

6 A slide in a playground is as shown in Fig. 46. The horizontal length of the slope is 4 m and the rise 2.8 m. Calculate the length of the slope itself.

Fig. 46

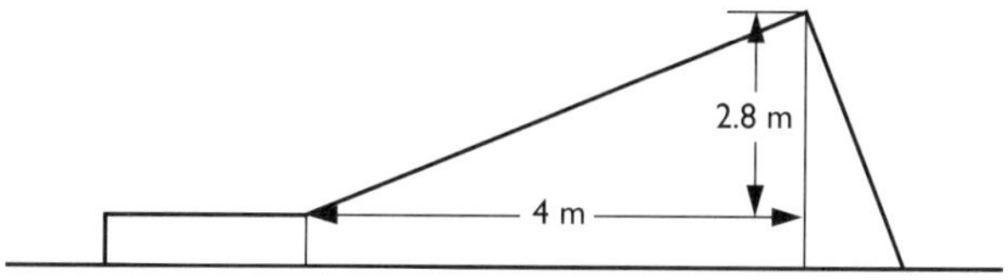

. . . .

. . . .

. . . .

7 Anne said that if the sides of a triangle were 13 cm, 12 cm and 4 cm, then it would be a right-angled triangle. Margaret said that it would not be a right-angled triangle. Who is correct, and why?

. . . .

. . . .

. . . .

. . . .

8 A square of side length 9 cm is drawn inside a circle as shown in Fig. 47.

Fig. 47

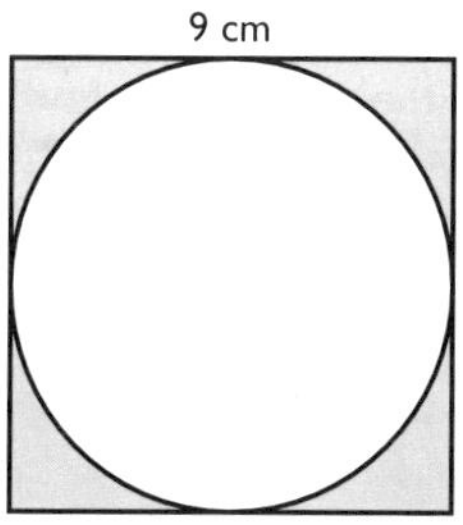

(a) Calculate the radius of the circle.

. . . .

. . . .

. . . .

(b) Calculate the area of the shaded part of the diagram.

. . . .

. . . .

. . . .

9 (a) Figure 48 shows an isosceles triangle of base 12 mm and height 17 mm.

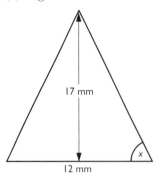

Fig. 48

(i) Calculate the area of the triangle.

....

....

(ii) Write down the value of tan *x*, giving your answer as a decimal.

....

....

(iii) Calculate the size of angle *x*.

....

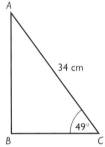

Fig. 49

(b) In the right-angled triangle *ABC* shown in Fig. 49, the hypotenuse *AC* is 34 cm, and the angle *ACB* is 49°. Calculate the length of the smallest side of the triangle.

....

....

....

....

10

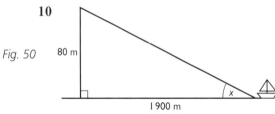

Fig. 50

The top of a vertical cliff is 80 m above sea level. At 9.30 a.m. a boat is 1900 m from the base of the cliff (Fig. 50).

(a) Calculate the angle of elevation of the top of the cliff from the boat.

....

....

....

(b) At 9.40 a.m. the angle of elevation of the top of the cliff from the boat is 11°. How far from the foot of the cliff is the boat?

....

....

....

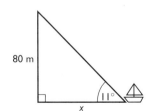

Fig. 51

(c) At what speed is the boat sailing towards the land?

....

....

Geometry and construction

TOPIC OUTLINE AND REVISION TIPS

Angles

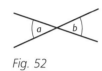

Fig. 52

Vertically opposite angles

The angles marked vertically opposite to each other in Fig. 52 are equal. The angles labelled a and b are vertically opposite angles.

Fig. 53

Angles on a line

The angles on a straight line add up to $180°$, i.e. in Fig. 53

$x + y + z = 180°$

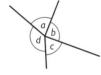

Fig. 54

Angles around a point

The sum of the angles around a point is $360°$, i.e. in Fig. 54

$a + b + c + d = 360°$

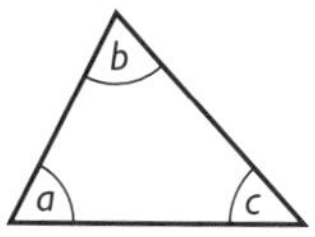

Fig. 55

Angles in a triangle

The three angles in a triangle all add up to $180°$ (Fig. 55).

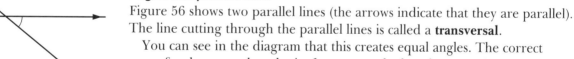

Angles and parallel lines

Figure 56 shows two parallel lines (the arrows indicate that they are parallel). The line cutting through the parallel lines is called a **transversal**.

You can see in the diagram that this creates equal angles. The correct name for these equal angles is **alternate** angles but they are often called Z angles since that is what they look like.

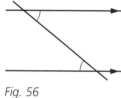

Fig. 56

This situation is also seen in Fig. 57, where the two angles shown will add up to $180°$. The two angles like this are called **allied** angles.

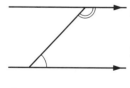

Fig. 57

Angles in a polygon

► Interior angles

For an N-sided polygon, the interior angles will add up to $180 \times (N - 2)$

► Regular polygons

Regular polygons are those that have every interior angle equal and each side the same length.
  – The exterior angle and the interior angle add up to $180°$.
  – The exterior angle of a regular N-sided polygon $= 360 \div N$.
  – The interior angle of a regular N-sided polygon $= 180° -$ exterior angle
$$= 180° - (360 \div N)$$

Example 1

What is the angle sum of a regular 9-sided polygon?

angle sum $= 180 \times (9 - 2) = 1260°$

Example 2

What are the sizes of the exterior and the interior angles of a regular polygon with 12 sides?

Exterior angle $= 360° \div 12 = 30°$

Interior angle $= 180° - 30° = 150°$

Bearing

Bearings are to help you find directions. There are two different types of bearing, as we show you below.

Compass bearings

The compass in Fig. 58a has all the bearings that you need to be familiar with.

Three-figure bearings

The compass in Fig. 58b is like the first one but with the three-figure bearings added. They are the angles measured clockwise from North, and the important ones to remember are the points North (000), East (090), South (180) and West (270).

Fig. 58

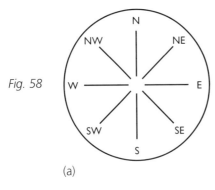

(a)

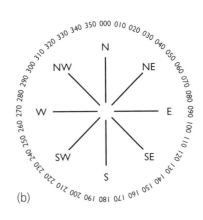

(b)

Special triangles

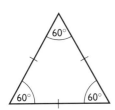

Fig. 59

Equilateral triangle

An equilateral triangle has all its sides the same length and each of its interior angles are 60° (Fig. 59).

Isosceles triangle

An isosceles triangle has two of its sides the same length and two of its angles are equal (Fig. 60).

Special quadrilaterals

Fig. 60

Trapezium

▶ A trapezium (Fig. 61) has one pair of opposite sides parallel.
▶ The angles at the same end of the parallel lines will add up to 180°.

Fig. 61

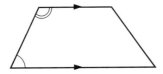

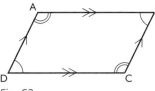
Fig. 62

Parallelogram

▶ A parallelogram (Fig. 62) has both opposite sides parallel.
▶ The opposite sides are equal in length.
▶ The diagonals of a parallelogram bisect each other.
▶ The opposite angles of a parallelogram are equal to each other, i.e. $\angle A = \angle C$ and $\angle B = \angle D$.

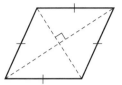
Fig. 63

Rhombus

▶ A rhombus (Fig. 63) is a parallelogram with all its sides the same length.
▶ The diagonals of a rhombus bisect each other at right angles.
▶ The diagonals of a rhombus bisect the angles.

Fig. 64

Kite

▶ A kite (Fig. 64) is a quadrilateral with two pairs of equal adjacent sides.
▶ The longer diagonal bisects the other diagonal at right angles.
▶ The angles between the different lengths are equal.

Congruency

Any shapes that are identical to each other in size and angles are said to be congruent to each other.

Example
The triangles shown in Fig. 65 are all congruent.

Fig. 65
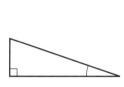  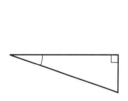 

Notice that the triangles can be in various orientations (positions).

For *triangles*, any one of the following four pieces of information is sufficient to indicate that the triangles are congruent:

▶ All sides are the same, known as SSS (side, side, side). See Fig. 66.

Fig. 66
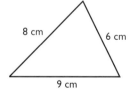 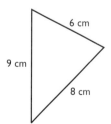

▶ Two sides and the angle between are equal, known as SAS (side, angle, side). See Fig. 67.

Fig. 67
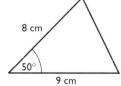 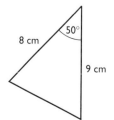

▶ Two angles and a corresponding side are equal, known as ASA (angle, side, angle). See Fig. 68.

Fig. 68

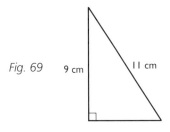 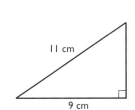

▶ Both triangles have a right angle with equal hypotenuse and other side, known as RHS (right angle, hypotenuse, side). See Fig. 69.

Fig. 69

Transformations

The particular change of position of shapes that you need to be familiar with are **translation**, **reflection**, **rotation** and **enlargement**.

All of these changes, except enlargement, keep a shape congruent but change its position.

Translation

A translation is a movement of a shape from one place to another without reflecting or rotating it.

We describe these changes of position using column vectors, which are a description of how to move from one point to another using horizontal shift and vertical shift.

Example

Fig. 70

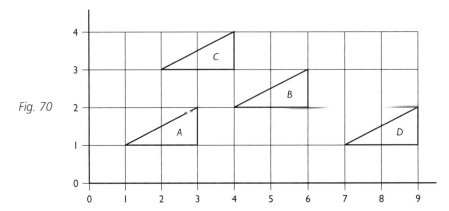

The vector describing the translation from *A* to *B* in Fig. 70 is $\begin{pmatrix} 3 \\ 1 \end{pmatrix}$

The vector describing the translation from *B* to *C* is $\begin{pmatrix} -2 \\ 1 \end{pmatrix}$

The vector describing the translation from B to D is $\begin{pmatrix} 3 \\ -1 \end{pmatrix}$

The vector describing the translation from D to A is $\begin{pmatrix} -6 \\ 0 \end{pmatrix}$

Notice that:

▶ the top number describes the horizontal movement; a minus sign means move left
▶ the bottom number describes the vertical movement; a minus sign means move down

Reflection

A reflection is what you see when you look in a mirror at right angles to it.

Example

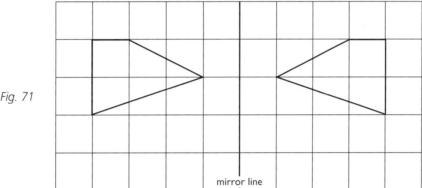

Fig. 71

Note that the line joining each point to its reflection is perpendicular to the mirror line.

Note: If you 'fold' over the mirror line then any point and its reflection should be on top of each other.

Rotations

A rotation of a shape is that shape turned, as a whole, around some particular point called the **centre of rotation**.

Example

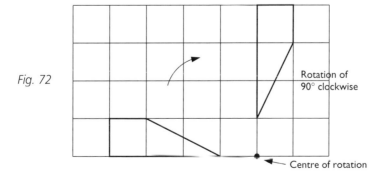

Fig. 72

Notice that:

▶ the angle given has direction, usually indicated by clockwise or anticlockwise
▶ the centre of rotation is always specified, in Fig. 72 it is by the dot
▶ the most common exam rotations are 90° and 180° around the origin

Enlargement

An enlargement always has a **centre of enlargement**, and a **scale factor**. Every length of the enlargement will be

> Original length × Scale factor

The distance of each image point on the enlargement from the centre of enlargement will be

> Distance from original point to centre of enlargement × Scale factor

There are two distinct ways to find an enlargement: the **ray method** and the **coordinate method**.

▶ Ray method
This is the way to find the enlargement if the diagram is not on a grid.

Example
An enlargement of scale factor 2 of triangle *ABC* in Fig. 73 from the centre of enlargement.

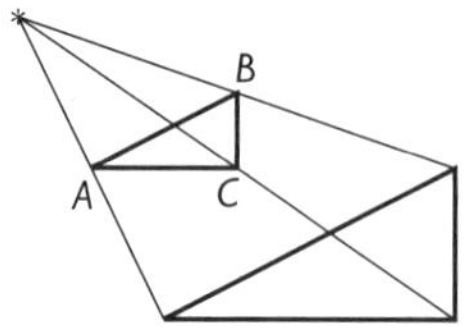

▶ Coordinate method
This is perhaps the easier way to enlarge a shape.

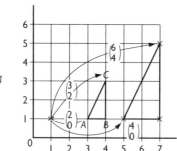

Fig. 73

Example
An enlargement of scale factor 2 of triangle *ABC* in Fig. 74 from the centre of enlargement.

Fig. 74

Bisectors

A bisector is something that divides something equally into two halves.

Constructing a line bisector
▶ Start with a line.
▶ Arc your pair of compasses at about three-quarters of the length of the line.
▶ From each end of the line draw two intersecting arcs without changing the radius of your compasses (Fig. 75).
▶ Join up where the two arcs cross (Fig. 76). The line you have just drawn bisects the original line and is known as the **perpendicular bisector**. You can use this same technique to construct a 90° angle.

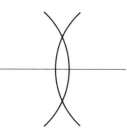

Fig. 75

Constructing an angle bisector
▶ Start with an angle.
▶ Arc your compasses at any reasonable radius that is smaller than the two lines.

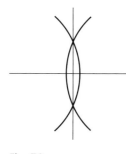

Fig. 76

- From the vertex of the angle, arc through both lines (Fig. 77).
- The compass can stay the same radius or be made longer now if need be. You have to make an arc from where each line of the angle intersects the initial arc (Fig. 78).
- Draw a line from where these two arcs cross to the vertex of the angle (Fig. 79). This line is the **angle bisector**, it has bisected the angle, i.e. cut it in half.

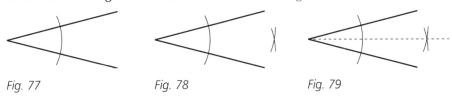

| Fig. 77 | Fig. 78 | Fig. 79 |

Constructing an angle of 60°

An angle of 60° is usually wanted at the end of a line, so we will assume that this is where it is wanted now.

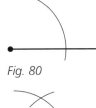

Fig. 80

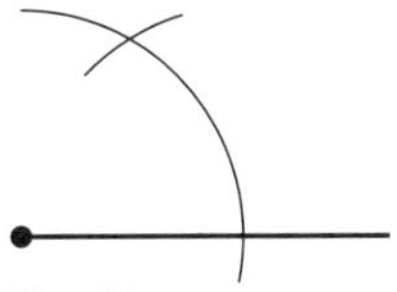

- Arc your compasses at about 3 cm.
- From the point on the line, arc from above through the line (Fig. 80).
- From where you have just arced through the line, arc from the end of the line through to the arc previously drawn (Fig. 81).

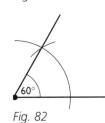

Fig. 81

- Join up the point of intersection to the point on the line: you have an angle of 60° (Fig. 82).

  Exam Hint: If the question says '*Construct*' then you must use compasses only, with no protractor. If it says '*Draw*' then use whatever you can to get an accurate diagram. Note though that, even when constructing, you can use your protractor to check your accuracy.

Fig. 82

Loci

A locus (plural *loci*) is the movement of a point according to a rule.

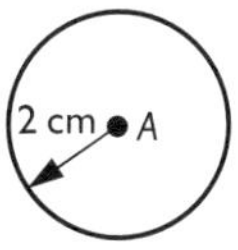

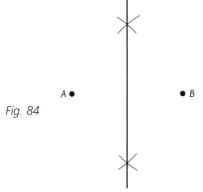

Fig. 83

Example 1

A point that moves so that it is at a distance of 2 cm from a fixed point, A, will have a locus that is a circle of radius 2 cm (Fig. 83).

If we express this mathematically we would say: the locus of the point P such that $AP = 2$ cm.

Example 2

A point moves so that it is always the same distance from two fixed points A and B. This will be the perpendicular bisector of the line AB (Fig. 84).

If we express this mathematically we would say: the locus of the point P such that $AP = BP$.

Fig. 84

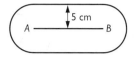

Fig. 85

Example 3
A point that moves so that it is always 5 cm from a line *AB* will have a 'sausage' or 'racetrack' shape around the line (Fig. 85).

Practical problems

Most problems that you get at GCSE are of a practical nature.

Example
A radio company wants to find a site for a transmitter. It wants the transmitter to be the same distance from Bawly and Littledale but within 20 miles of Stanton.

Translated into mathematical language, this means the perpendicular bisector between Littledale and Bawly and the area within a circle of radius 20 miles from Stanton. The map in Fig. 86 is drawn to a scale of 1 cm = 10 miles.

Fig. 86

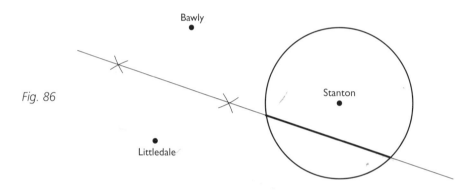

So the transmitter can be built anywhere along the thick black line.

Symmetry of two-dimensional shapes

Lines of symmetry
A way to recognise a line of symmetry is to see if the shape can be folded on the line of symmetry so that both halves fall exactly on top of each other.
   Look at the shapes in Fig. 87. The lines of symmetry are marked by a dashed line.

Fig. 87

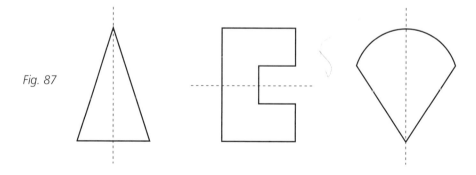

Rotational symmetry
A flat shape has rotational symmetry if it can be rotated about a point in such a way that it looks just the same in the new position.
   Look at the shapes in Fig. 88. They each have rotational symmetry as you can rotate them about the dot so that they look the same in another position. This dot is called the **point of symmetry**.

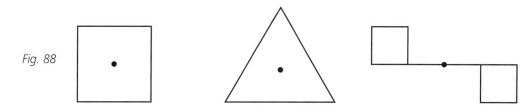

Fig. 88

The **order of rotational symmetry** of any shape is given by the number of different positions in which the shape looks the same after it has been rotated about its point of symmetry (like the centre of rotation in transformation geometry).

Examples
▶ A parallelogram has rotational symmetry of order 2.
▶ A regular hexagon has rotational symmetry of order 6.

Note that *every* shape has an *order* of symmetry but a shape only has *rotational* symmetry if its order is 2 or higher.

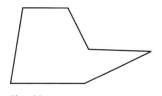

Fig. 89

Example
The shape shown in Fig. 89 has no symmetry at all yet we say it has rotational symmetry of order 1. Nevertheless, we still say that it has *no* symmetry.

Tessellations
Tessellations are another form of symmetry within plane flat surfaces. A tessellation is a regular pattern made with just one shape in such a way that it would fill the whole of a huge flat surface so that no gaps are left (except perhaps at the edges).

Example

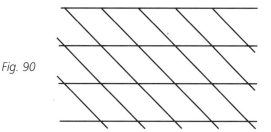

Fig. 90

Figure 90 is an example of a tessellation.

Solid three-dimensional shapes

A good way to draw a solid shape is by using an isometric grid, as in Fig. 91.

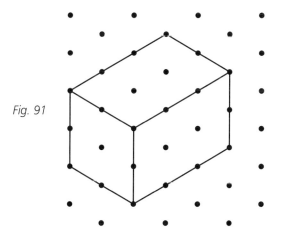

Fig. 91

Nets of solid shapes

A net of a solid shape is the shape drawn out onto a piece of paper or card in such a way that if you cut round the whole shape you could fold it up into the solid shape.

Example
Figure 92 shows a net of a cuboid.

Fig. 92

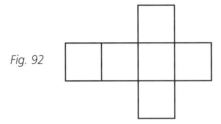

This net could be folded up into a cuboid. (Note that if you intended to make this into a cuboid then you would have to put little tabs on some sides to be able to glue the thing together. For examination question involving nets, though, you do *not* need to put the tabs on.)

Symmetry of three-dimensional shapes

Planes of symmetry

This concept is like lines of symmetry on flat shapes but also involves depth. Solid shapes have **planes of symmetry**: they are where you can slice a solid shape into two equal halves where again one half is the reflection of the other in that plane.

Rotational symmetry

This is like the rotational symmetry of flat shapes but again the depth is there which makes the point of symmetry become a line, which we call the **axis of symmetry**.

A solid shape has an axis of symmetry if the shape can rotate about that axis and looks as if it is still in the original place.

REVISION ACTIVITY

Complete the following.

1 Write down the name of each angle.
   (a) Less than 90°   (b) Between 90° and 180°
   (c) Between 180° and 360°   (d) Equal to 90°
2 Write down a formula for each of the following in a regular polygon of
   N sides,
   (a) exterior angle   (b) interior angle.
3 What solid shape could be drawn from each of the nets shown in Fig. 93?

Fig. 93

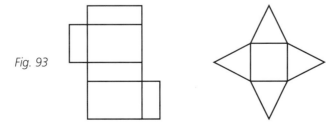

4 Complete the sentence. 'Two shapes are congruent if...'
5 Draw in the lines of symmetry for each of the shapes in Fig. 94.

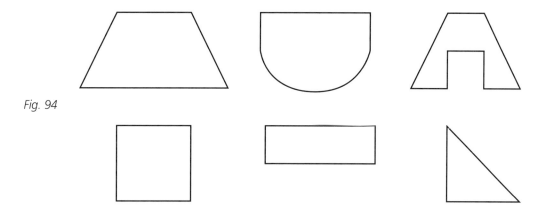

Fig. 94

6 Write down the order of rotational symmetry for each of the shapes in Fig. 95.

a)   b)   c)

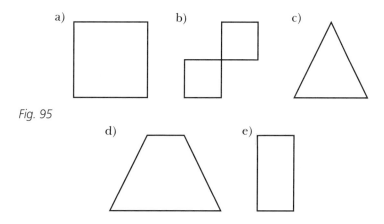

Fig. 95

d)   e)

7 Construct the perpendicular bisector of the line *AB* in Fig. 96.

Fig. 96   A ——————————————— B

8 Construct the angle bisector of the angle *ABC* in Fig. 97.

Fig. 97
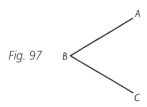

9 Construct a right-angled triangle *ABC*, where $B = 90°$, $C = 60°$ and $BC = 5$ cm.

10 On the grid in Fig. 98 draw the position of the shaded shape after:

(a) a translation of $\begin{pmatrix} 3 \\ 2 \end{pmatrix}$

(b) a reflection in the *x*-axis

(c) a rotation of $90°$ anticlockwise about the origin

(d) an enlargement of scale factor 2 from point (4, 6)

Fig. 98
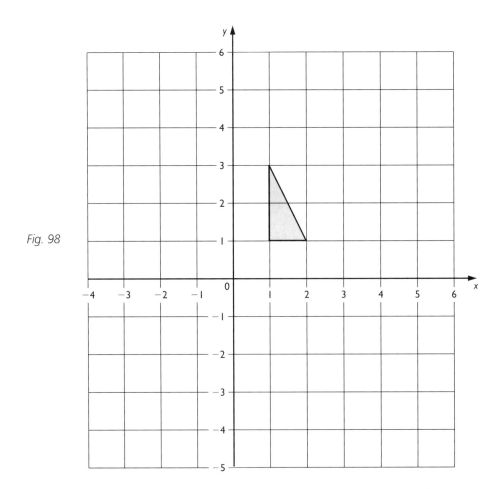

1

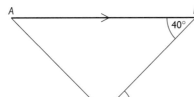

Fig. 99

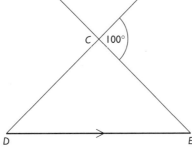

(a) Work out the size of angle *BDE* in Fig. 99 giving a reason for your answer.

....

....

(b) Work out the size of angle *BAE* in Fig. 99 giving a reason for your answer.

....

....

2 Figure 100 represents a regular nonagon with two of its lines of symmetry shown.

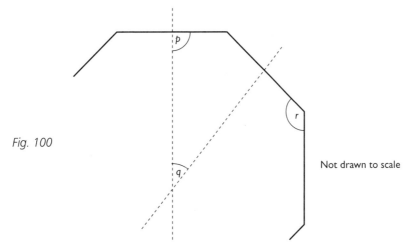

Fig. 100

Not drawn to scale

(a) Write down the value of angle *p*.

....

(b) Calculate the size of angle:

　　(i) *q*　...

　　(ii) *r*　...

3

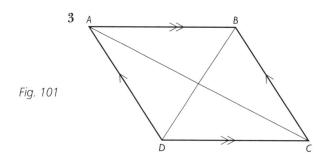

Fig. 101

Which triangle in Fig. 101 is congruent to *ABC*? State why.

....

4

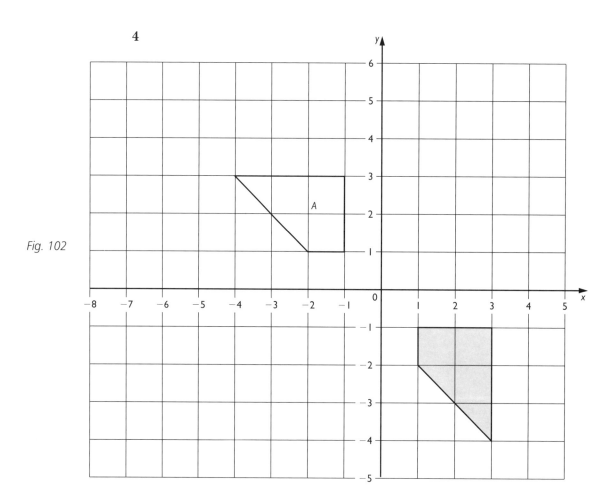

Fig. 102

(a) Describe fully the single transformation that will transform the shape
   labelled *A* in Fig. 102 to the shaded shape.

   ....

(b) On the grid in Fig. 102 draw the shape labelled *A* after it has been
   rotated 90° clockwise about the origin. Label it *B*.
(c) On the same grid, enlarge the shape labelled *A* by a scale factor of 2 from
   the centre of enlargement *P*(−1, 6).

5

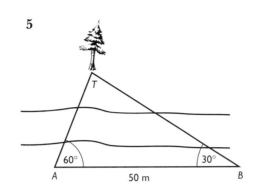

Fig. 103

I want to find out how far away a tree (*T*) is on the other side of a river. I mark out a baseline, *AB*, 50 metres long as shown on Fig. 103. I now measure the angles at the ends *A* and *B* between the baseline and the lines of sight of the tree. These angles are 30° and 60°.

Using ruler and compasses only make a scale drawing, find the shortest distance of the tree (*T*) from the baseline *AB*. Use a scale of 1 cm to 10 m.

6 The solid shape shown in Fig. 104 falls over onto the shaded face. On the same grid, draw the shape after it has fallen over.

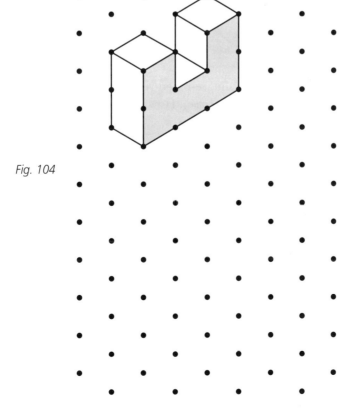

Fig. 104

7 Figure 105 shows a cuboid with a volume of 36 cm³. Sketch another cuboid with different lengths that also has a volume of 36 cm³.

Fig. 105

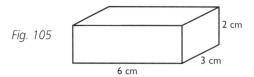

2 cm

3 cm

6 cm

8 A builder is putting a square piece of plane glass into a window.
His daughter says, 'There are four ways you can put that in.'
The man replies, 'No there's not, there are . . .'.
(a) Complete what the builder could correctly say.

. . . .

(b) Give clear reasons to justify your answer.

. . . .

. . . .

9

Fig. 106

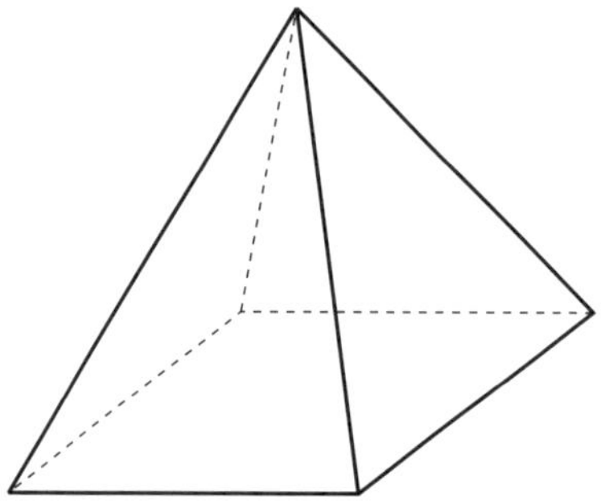

Figure 106 shows a square-based right pyramid (i.e., the vertex is directly above the centre of the base). How many planes of symmetry does it have?

. . . .

10

Fig. 107

X •

• Y

Figure 107 shows a town with two schools *X* and *Y*. Pupils are told to go to the school nearest to them. Shade the region of the town from which pupils go to school *X*.

11 Draw and write down what you know about the properties of each shape.

(a) Isosceles ....

....

....

(b) Equilateral triangle ....

....

....

(c) Parallelogram ....

....

....

(d) Trapezium ....

....

....

12 A new TV mast is to provide services for the three towns Amylle, Brum and Cheal. The diagram is drawn to a scale of 1 cm to 10 km.

The mast is to be put inside the triangle by Amylle and Brum and 30 km from Cheal. Construct the position of the mast on the diagram, label its position.

Probability and statistics

TOPIC OUTLINE AND REVISION TIPS

Averages

▶ The **mode** is the item of data that occurs the most.
▶ The **median** is the item in the middle once all the data have been put in order of size. If we have an even set of numbers, we have to find the middle two numbers: the median is then halfway between these two middle numbers (easiest to find by adding these two numbers and dividing by 2).
▶ The **mean** is the result found by adding all the data together and dividing the total by how many items of data you started with.
▶ The **range** is the difference between the highest and lowest number in the data.

Example
From 1, 1, 3, 4, 5, 5, 5, 5, 6, 6, 7, 8, 9, 11, 13, 15, 15, 17, 17, 18, 25

▶ The *mode* is 5 since this occurs four times (more than any other).
▶ The *median* is 7 since this item is the middle item of data.
▶ The *mean* is 9.3 since when the items are added and divided by the number of items you get $196 \div 21$ which is 9.3 (1 d.p.).
▶ The *range* is 24 since the largest number, 25, minus the smallest number, 1, is 24.

Frequency tables

When a lot of information has been gathered it is convenient to put it together in a frequency table. From this you can then find what the various averages are.

Example
A survey was done on the number of people in cars using a particular motorway service station. The results are summarised in the table below.

Number of people	1	2	3	4	5	6
Frequency		12	46	138	95	37	11

(a) The modal number of people in the cars is easy to see: it is the number with the largest frequency, i.e. 138. Hence the modal number in the cars was 3.
(b) The median number of people in the cars is found by working out where the middle is. We can add up the frequency to get 339 cars that were surveyed. This gives the middle position $(339 + 1) \div 2$ which is 170.

   We now need to count the frequencies along the table until we find which group the 170th car is in. This is found in the group with 3 in the car. So the median number of people in a car is 3.

(c) The mean number of people in a car is to be found by adding all the people together and dividing by the number of cars. This is set out in the following table.

Number in the car	Frequency	Number in these cars
1	12	1 × 12 = 12
2	46	2 × 46 = 92
3	138	3 × 138 = 414
4	95	4 × 95 = 380
5	37	5 × 37 = 185
6	11	6 × 11 = 66
Totals	339	1149

The mean is found by $1149 \div 339 = 3.4$ (rounded)
Hence the mean number of people in a car is 3.4

Grouped data

Sometimes the information we are given is grouped together as in the **grouped frequency table** below which shows the range of values for pocket money found in a survey of 25 children of a given age.

Pocket money (£)	0.00–1.00	1.01–2.00	2.01–3.00	3.01–4.00	4.01–5.00
No. of children	2	7	12	3	1

The *modal group* is the one with the largest frequency, which is £2.01–£3.00.

The *median* will be in the middle of a group and one way to find it is to draw a particular type of graph called a **cumulative curve**.

The *mean* can only be estimated since we do not have all the information we need for an accurate calculation. To estimate the mean we simply assume that each person in each group has the 'midway' amount and we build up a table as below.

Note how we find the mid-way value. We add the two end values together and divide by 2. We could round this off to the nearest penny if we wished since it is only an estimate, but it is usual not to do this rounding until the very last moment.

Pocket money	Frequency (f)	Midway (m)	$f \times m$	Total
0.00–1.00	2	0.50	2 × 0.50	1.00
1.01–2.00	7	1.505	7 × 1.505	10.535
2.01–3.00	12	2.505	12 × 2.505	30.06
3.01–4.00	3	3.505	3 × 3.505	10.515
4.01–5.00	1	4.505	1 × 4.505	4.505
Total	25			56.615

The estimated mean will be £56.615 ÷ 25 = £2.26 (2 d.p.).

You will come across a few different ways of labelling the groups in a grouped frequency table. For example, the above table might have been labelled

Pocket money (£p)	$0 \leqslant p \leqslant 1$	$1 < p \leqslant 2$	$2 < p \leqslant 3$	$3 < p \leqslant 4$	$4 < p \leqslant 5$

in which $2 < p \leqslant 3$ is read as 'pocket money is more than £2 but less than or equal to £3', and so on.

You will see different ways of using the inequalities in a grouped frequency table. It will make little difference to the middle value as you still use the average of the end points.

Charts

Statistical information is often presented in chart form such as

▶ frequency polygons,
▶ bar charts and histograms,
▶ pie charts.

Frequency polygons
Information given in a table, as below, gives a simple frequency polygon.

Example 1

Patients	1	2	3	4	5
Frequency	10	19	20	17	6

The frequency polygon looks like that in Fig. 108.

Fig. 108

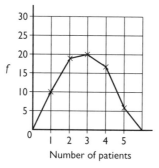

Notice:

▶ How we simply plot the coordinate from each ordered pair in the table.
▶ How we start and finish the polygon by coming down to 0 on the frequency axis one unit back and one unit on from the start and end respectively.

Example 2

Patients	1–10	11–20	21–30	31–40	41–50
Frequency	3	21	35	29	11

The frequency polygon looks like that in Fig. 109.

Notice:

▶ How we use the midpoint of each group, just as we did in estimating the mean.
▶ How we plot the ordered pairs of midpoints with frequency, i.e. (5.5, 3), (15.5, 21), (25.5, 35), (35.5, 29), (45.5, 11)
▶ How we again start and finish the polygon at points where the frequency is 0: we use the points on the horizontal axis keeping the same horizontal distance between the other midpoints. In other words (-4.5, 0) and (55.5, 0) are the respective end points of the polygon.

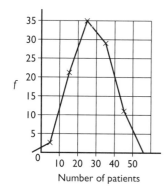

Fig. 109

Histogram

A histogram looks similar to a bar chart but with three fundamental differences:

▶ There are no gaps between the bars.
▶ The horizontal axis uses a continuous scale since it is used mainly for continuous data such as time, weight or length.
▶ The area of each bar represents the frequency.

All the histograms that you will meet in the intermediate level of GCSE will be used only for continuous data such as weight, length or time, and they will use equal-width histograms, hence the relative heights of the bars will represent the frequency.

If the data are not continuous – for example, scores in a test or goals scored by a team – then a simple bar chart will be used.

Look at the histogram in Fig. 110 which is drawn from this table of times taken to do a particular job measured to the nearest minute.

Time (minutes)	1–3	4–6	7–9	10–12
Frequency (f)	7	11	5	4

Fig. 110

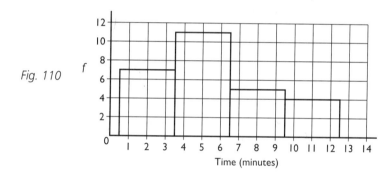

Notice that the histogram bars start and finish at the least possible and greatest possible times for *each* group. Take, for example the time region 4–6 minutes: the least possible time is $3\frac{1}{2}$ minutes and the greatest possible time is $6\frac{1}{2}$ minutes.

Because the widths are all the same, then the heights can be used to represent the frequency.

Pie charts

Example
Draw a pie chart to illustrate the following information.

Destination	UK	America	Asia	Europe	Africa
Frequency	165	23	13	75	21

We need to find the fraction of 360 that each type of transport represents. This is usually done in a table like the following.

Destination	Frequency	Calculation	Angle
UK	165	$\frac{165}{297} \times 360$	$\approx 200°$
America	23	$\frac{23}{297} \times 360$	$\approx 28°$
Asia	13	$\frac{13}{297} \times 360$	$\approx 16°$
Europe	75	$\frac{75}{297} \times 360$	$\approx 91°$
Africa	21	$\frac{21}{297} \times 360$	$\approx 25°$
Total	297		360°

Notes:

► You use the total frequency (297) to calculate each fraction.
► You round off each angle to the nearest degree.
► You check that all the angles do add up to 360°.

The pie chart can now be drawn. Remember that it is always good practice to draw the smallest angles first, then the next smallest and so on until the last angle, which will be the largest. This is so that the errors that inevitably accumulate to the last angle have the least visible effect on the angle shown.

Surveys

A survey is an organised way of asking a lot of people a few well constructed questions, or making a lot of observations in an experiment in order to reach a conclusion about something.

Simple data collection sheet

If you need simply to collect some data for analysis then you want to design a simple data capture sheet.

Example
'Which day of the week do you want to go on the school trip at the end of term?'

You can ask a lot of pupils and put the results straight onto a data capture sheet like that below.

	Tally	Total
Sunday	III	3
Monday	JHT JHT II	12
Tuesday	JHT JHT IIII	14
Wednesday	JHT III	8
Thursday	JHT JHT JHT III	18
Friday	JHT JHT JHT JHT JHT JHT JHT JHT JHT JHT JHT II	57
Saturday	JHT III	8
Don't mind	JHT JHT JHT JHT II	22

Notice how we made space for tally marks, and note how we *gate* the tallies to give groups of fives which make it easier to count up once the survey is complete.

This is a good simple data collection sheet since only one question is involved and each person asked can easily be given a tally on the sheet before moving on to the next person.

Questionnaires

When asking questions on a questionnaire you have to be careful to note the following points:

▶ Never ask leading questions designed to get a particular response.
▶ Never ask personal or irrelevant questions.
▶ Always keep the questions as simple as possible.
▶ Always set a question that will get a response from whoever is asked.

The following types of questions are **bad** questions and should not appear on any of your questionnaires:

▶ 'What is your age?' This is personal, many will not want to answer.
▶ 'Slaughtering animals to test cosmetics is cruel to the poor defenceless animal, don't you agree?' This is a leading question, designed to get a 'yes'.
▶ 'Do you fly when you go abroad?' This can be answered only by those people who have been abroad.
▶ 'If you are in town one day and you see a person asking for some money because he looks homeless, do you feel sorry for him and give him some money or do you tell him where to get some help from?' This is a rather complicated question.

The following types of question are **good** questions in contrast to the poor ones above.

▶ In which age group are you?
  0–20   21–30   31–50   over 50
▶ Do you think it is cruel to kill animals in order to test cosmetics?
▶ If you went abroad would you fly?
▶ Would you give money to a person begging in the street?

A questionnaire is usually put together to test a hypothesis or a statement made by someone.

Example
'People who live in Yorkshire are the only ones who like Yorkshire puddings with treacle on.'

Design a questionnaire that can be used to test if this statement is true or not.

The questions we need to include are:

▶ Do you live in Yorkshire?
▶ Do you eat Yorkshire puddings?
▶ If you eat Yorkshire puddings, do you put treacle on?

Once these questions have been answered then they can be looked at to see if the statement is true or not.

Scatter diagram

A scatter diagram (or scattergram) is a graph that plots quite a few points representing *two* things. It is used to see if there is any connection between those two things. This connection is called a **correlation**.

Example
The scatter graphs in Figs 111–113 represent the three different types of correlation that can be found.

1. Do taller people have bigger feet?

Fig. 111   Height
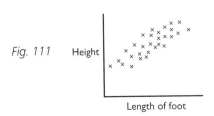
Length of foot

Figure 111 shows positive (or direct) correlation. In this case it shows that the taller people are, the larger their feet are likely to be.

2. Is there a connection between temperature and the number of scarves sold?

Fig. 112   Number of scarves sold
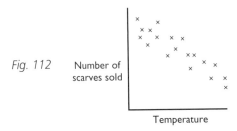
Temperature

Figure 112 shows negative (or indirect) correlation. Here it shows that the higher the temperature, the fewer scarves that are likely to be sold.

3. Is there a connection between weight and pocket money for Y11 students?

Fig. 113   Pocket money
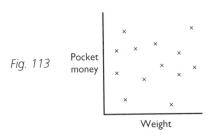
Weight

Figure 113 shows no correlation, i.e. there is no connection between weight and pocket money for Y11 students.

Lines of best fit
If we see there is a correlation between two things then we can draw a line of best fit, that is a line that follows the trend of the plotted data (Fig. 114).

Fig. 114   Height
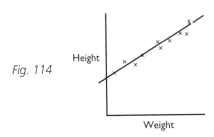
Weight

When you draw this line of best fit you should be trying to:

▶ Show the trend
▶ Have as many points above the line as below it.
▶ Draw the line from one side of the available graph to the other.

But beware:

▶ This line does *not* have to go through all the points.
▶ This line does *not* have to go through the origin.
▶ This line is *not* drawn from the first to the last point.
▶ This line is usually straight but it could be curved. (However until you get to A-level statistics all the lines of best fit you will meet should be straight lines.)

Cumulative frequency

Cumulative frequency is what is commonly called *running totals*. It is used to draw a cumulative frequency diagram, from which we can estimate the median as well as find quartiles.

Example

You will see that the following frequency table has had a cumulative frequency column added and that there is a running total.

Score	Frequency	Cumulative frequency
1–20	5	5
21–40	9	14
41–60	18	32
61–80	41	73
81–100	19	92

This running total can now be plotted onto a cumulative frequency diagram which could be either a curve or a polygon. Each one has been drawn for you in Fig. 115. Notice the difference.

▶ The cumulative frequency curve has a smooth curve (called the **ogive**).
▶ The cumulative frequency polygon uses straight lines between each point.

Both are used, and since the whole diagram is an approximation it will make little difference as to which one you choose, unless of course you were asked to do one particular type in an exam.

Fig. 115

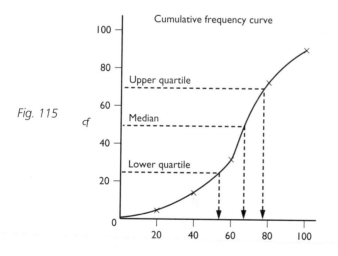
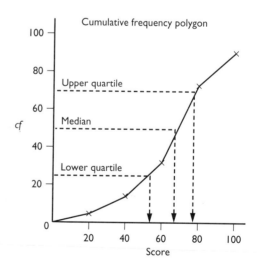

From these graphs we can read off:

▶ Median = 68 marks, Upper quartile = 77 marks, Lower quartile = 52 marks
▶ Interquartile range = (77 − 52) = 25
▶ Semi interquartile range = 12.5

Notice how you can find the **median** by looking halfway along the frequency, and the **quartiles** come at the quarter marks. The **interquartile range** is the difference between the upper and the lower quartiles.

Probability

The definition of probability is

$$P(\text{event}) = \frac{\text{Number of ways the event can happen}}{\text{Total number of outcomes}}$$

This definition always leads to a fraction. If possible the fraction should be cancelled down.

Experimental probability

This can be found by performing an experiment or making an observation many times, and keeping an accurate record of the results. The experimental probability of a particular event happening can then be worked out as:

$$\text{Experimental probability} = \frac{\text{Number of times the event has happened}}{\text{Total number of observations}}$$

Example
A balanced die was rolled 100 times. The number 2 occurred a total of 21 times. This gives an experimental probability of

$$\frac{21}{100} = 0.21$$

Theoretical probability

This is found by considering equally likely events. Equally likely events are those that all have an equal chance of happening.

For example, equally likely events are those like rolling a die and getting a 1, 2, 3, 4, 5 or 6. Whereas, events that are *not* equally likely are those like rolling two dice and getting the totals 2, 3, 4, 5, 6, 7, etc.

The theoretical probability of an event is found by the fraction

$$\text{Theoretical probability} = \frac{\text{Number of ways the event can happen}}{\text{Total number of different equally likely events that can occur}}$$

Examples
► Probability of rolling a dice and getting a $4 = \frac{1}{6}$
► Probability of tossing a coin and getting a head $= \frac{1}{2}$

Expectation

The expectation of an event happening is found by multiplying the probability of the event by how many times the event has the opportunity of happening.

Example
I cut a pack of cards 200 times. How many times would I expect to get a king?

The expectation will be

$$200 \times \frac{4}{52} = 15 \quad \text{(rounded)}$$

Probability of not happening

The probability of an event *not* happening is found by subtracting from 1 the probability of it happening.

Example
The probability of snow in March is 0.15.
The probability of *no* snow in March will be $1 - 0.15 = 0.85$

Or *rule*

If two events, A and B, are mutually exclusive (i.e. they cannot both happen at the same time), then the probability of event A **or** B happening is the probability of A happening *added* to the probability of B happening. This can be written as

$$P(A \text{ or } B) = P(A) + P(B)$$

Example

Four brothers have a race.

▶ The probability of Kevin winning is 0.2
▶ The probability of Brian winning is 0.4
▶ The probability of Malcolm winning is 0.25
▶ The probability of David winning is 0.15

What is the probability of either Kevin or Malcolm winning?

The events are mutually exclusive so we add their probabilities

Probability of Kevin or Malcolm winning $= 0.2 + 0.25 = 0.45$

Independent events

If two events can happen at the same time then we say that the events are **independent**.

Examples
▶ Rolling two dice and getting a 4 then a 2.
▶ Being dealt two cards, a jack then a queen.

And *rule*

If we have two (or more) independent events happening, event A and event B, then the probability of event A happening **and** then event B happening is found by *multiplying* the probability of event A by the probability of event B. This can be written

$$P(A \text{ and } B) = P(A).P(B)$$

Example

The probability of Ammitt getting his homework all correct is 0.15
The probability of Rachel getting her homework all correct is 0.65
What is the probability of them *both* getting the homework right?

Both implies the *and* rule which means multiply the probabilities

Probability of both getting homework right $= 0.15 \times 0.65 = 0.0975$

Tree diagrams

A tree diagram can help us to see all the possibilities in a given situation and usually makes use of the *or* rule and the *and* rule in the same situation. Follow through the problem below that uses a tree diagram.

Example

Two cards are dealt out. What is the probability of

(a) both being spades?
(b) one being a spade?
(c) at least one being a spade?

The tree diagram is drawn as in Fig. 116, with the probabilities being put on the branches. Note the second set of probabilities depends on which card was chosen as the first card.

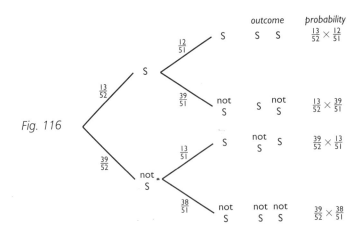

Fig. 116

The probabilities of the combined events have been calculated using the *and* rule.

(a) The probability of both being spades is $\dfrac{13}{52} \times \dfrac{12}{51} = \dfrac{156}{2652} = 0.06$ (rounded)

(b) The probability of one spade is either

$$\text{spade then no spade:} \quad \text{Probability} = \frac{13}{52} \times \frac{39}{51} = \frac{507}{2\,652}$$

or $$\text{no spade then a spade:} \quad \text{Probability} = \frac{39}{52} \times \frac{13}{51} = \frac{507}{2\,652}$$

So the probability of one *or* the other happening is found by *adding* their probabilities

$$\frac{507}{2\,652} + \frac{507}{2\,652} = \frac{1014}{2\,652} = 0.38 \text{ (rounded)}$$

(c) The probability of at least one being a spade can be found in two different ways:
   (i) This happens when either you get one spade *or* two spades, hence *add* their probabilities

   $$\frac{1014}{2\,652} + \frac{156}{2\,652} = \frac{1170}{2\,652} = 0.44$$

   (ii) We could see this is the probability of *avoiding* getting no spades at all; hence subtract from 1 the probability of no spade *and* no spade, which is

   $$1 - \frac{1482}{2\,652} = 0.44$$

It is useful to see both these two methods, as in different problems one method may well be more useful than the other.

★ REVISION ACTIVITY

Complete the following.

1 Name each type of average: (a) Most frequent item,   (b) Middle value once arranged in order,   (c) Total value divided by number of items.

2 Write down a list of 5 numbers that:
   (a) has a mode of 3
   (b) has a median of 4
   (c) has a mean of 5
3 Sketch a scatter diagram that has: (a) positive correlation, (b) negative correlation, (c) no correlation.
4 From the cumulative frequency diagram in Fig. 117, write down what is:
   (a) the median, (b) the lower quartile, (c) the upper quartile,
   (d) the interquartile range.

Fig. 117

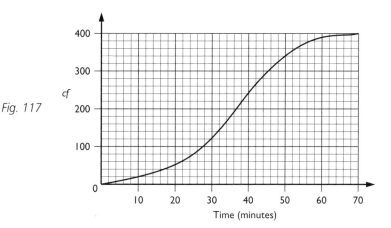

5 A bag contains 4 blue balls and 8 white balls. What are the probabilities of choosing the following from the bag?
   (a) a blue ball
   (b) a ball that is *not* blue
   (c) one blue ball, putting it back and then another blue ball
   (d) two blue balls at the same time
   (e) two balls of the same colour

PRACTICE QUESTIONS

1 The fifteen members of a rugby team were asked what size of boot they wore. The replies were

11, 12, 8, 13, 12, 11, 8, 10, 9, 11, 8, 12, 10, 9, 12

For these sizes, find:
(a) the mode   ....
(b) the median   ....
(c) the mean   ....
(d) the range   ....

2 At Murex's rental shop the number of items rented out in one week were:
Televisions   58
Videos   26
Computers   14
Other equipment   2
   (a) Write the number of videos as a fraction of the total sales.

   ....

(b) The manager decides to show these figures in a pie chart. Calculate the angle which represents the number of televisions sold.

....

....

....

3 All the Y11's took a spelling test. The table below shows the results.

Number of spellings correct x	Frequency
$0 \leqslant x < 20$	16
$20 \leqslant x < 30$	21
$30 \leqslant x < 40$	28
$40 \leqslant x < 50$	38
$50 \leqslant x < 60$	17
$60 \leqslant x < 100$	3
Total	123

(a) What is the modal class?

....

(b) Calculate an estimated mean number of correct spellings.

....

....

....

4 A teacher did a survey to find out what each of the 108 Y11 students had for lunch. The results are shown in the pie chart in Fig. 118.

Fig. 118

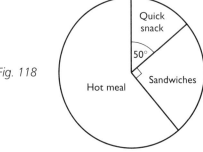

(a) Calculate how many of these 108 pupils
  (i) had sandwiches

....

  (ii) had a hot meal

....

....

(b) You have been asked to do a similar survey for the whole school. Design the observation sheet that you would use to collect the required information.

....

....

....

5 A marathon is held in Hope one year.

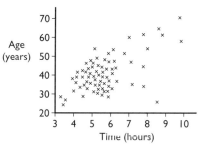

Fig. 119

(a) The scatter diagram in Fig. 119 shows the ages of these runners and the times they took to complete the marathon. What does the scatter diagram tell you?

....

(b) The table below shows the times taken by 50 men and 50 women

Time taken (t hours)	Men	Women
$2 < t \leqslant 3$	44	16
$3 < t \leqslant 4$	91	34
$4 < t \leqslant 5$	58	82
$5 < t \leqslant 6$	32	78
$6 < t \leqslant 7$	18	21
$7 < t \leqslant 8$	7	19

Draw a frequency polygon to show the distribution of times taken.

(c) The frequency polygon for the women's times is different from that for the men's times. Describe how they differ.

....

....

6 Helen and James played 40 games of golf together. The table below shows Helen's scores.

Scores (x)	$70 < x \leqslant 80$	$80 < x \leqslant 90$	$90 < x \leqslant 100$	$100 < x \leqslant 110$	$110 < x \leqslant 120$
Frequency	2	5	14	16	3

(a) Draw a cumulative frequency diagram to show Helen's scores.
(b) Use your graph to find:
   (i) Helen's median score

   ....

   (ii) the interquartile range of her scores

   ....

(c) James' median score was 102. The interquartile range of his score was 7.
   (i) Who was the more consistent player? Give a reason for your choice.

   ....

   (ii) The winner of a game of golf is the one with the lowest score. Who won most of these 40 games? Give a reason for your choice.

   ....

   ....

7 The school bus should pick up Wayne at 8.30 each morning. Sometimes the bus is early and he misses it. Describe how Wayne could estimate the probability of this bus being early.

....

....

....

....

8 Ben has bought 16 tickets for the Instant National Lottery. He wins a prize on one of them and says, 'This shows that the chances of winning a prize in the Instant National Lottery is $\frac{1}{16}$.'
(a) Is he correct?

....

(b) Give a reason for your answer.

....

....

9 In a game you throw two dice and add the two numbers showing. If you score 11 or more you win a prize.
(a) Copy and complete the table below to show all the possible outcomes for the game.

6	......	......	......	......	......	......
5	......	......	......	......	......	......
4	5	......	......	......	......	......
3	4	......	......	......	......	......
2	3	4	......	......	......	......
1	2	3	4	5	6	......
Dice	1	2	3	4	5	6

(b) What is the probability that you win a prize with one roll of the dice?

....

(c) At the fête, 400 people are expected to play the game once. Approximately how many prizes will be won?

....

10 A bag contains 15 toffees and 5 mints.
(a) What is the probability that a sweet taken from the bag at random will be a toffee?

....

(b) Another bag contains 9 jellies and 11 mints. One sweet is taken from each bag without looking. Complete a tree diagram to show the possible outcomes and their probabilities.
(c) What is the probability of taking
   (i) two mints?

....

   (ii) exactly one mint?

....

....

Solutions
Number

SOLUTIONS TO REVISION ACTIVITY

1 (a) 2, 3, 5, 7, 11, 13, 17, 19
　(b) 1, 4, 9, 16, 25, 36, 49, 64
2 (a) $2^4 \times 3^2$,　(b) $2^2 \times 5 \times 7$
3 (a) 8 995,　(b) 57
4 (a) 5.85 kg　(b) 3.95 m
5 10.85 kg (4 s.f.)
6 (a) 9.684×10^3,　(b) 5×10^4,　(c) 3.82×10^4,　(d) 9.5×10^{-3},
　(e) 8×10^6,　(f) 8.67×10^{-1}
7 (a) $40 \times 20 = 800$,　(b) $560 \div 7 = 80$,　(c) $(140 \times 60) \div 7 = 1\,200$
　(d) $8^2 + 10^2 \approx 60 + 100 = 160$
8 (a) 2.64,　(b) 1.34,　(c) 17.6,　(d) 7.5,　(e) 20,　(f) 0.006
9 £130 : £195
10 (a) 20.8% (rounded),　(b) 12.5%,　(c) 25%

ANSWERS TO PRACTICE QUESTIONS

1

$$\begin{array}{r} 13 \quad \text{r}\,28 \\ 44\overline{)600} \\ \underline{44} \\ 160 \\ \underline{132} \\ 28 \end{array}$$

Your answer is 13 full boxes with 28 programmes left over.

Examiner's note to get any marks here you have to show that you have worked this out without a calculator, as above. You score 1 mark for the method of dividing and 1 for the correct answer.

2 $\dfrac{700 \times 80}{40} = 700 \times 2 = 1\,400$

Examiner's note You get marks for rounding off to 1 s.f. and trying to change the numbers to make the division easier. You would score 1 mark for rounding to 1 s.f., 1 mark for rounding to something useful to help the division and 1 mark for a suitable estimate.

3 (a) 27 750,　(b) 27 849

Examiner's note You have to think what would round up and down to 27 800. Part (b) needs careful thinking about because often this correct upper limit is 27 850, but in the case of discrete actual digits this is not the case.
　You score 1 mark for each correct part (a) and (b).

4 £270 × 1.04 = £280.80　or　4% of £270 = 270 × 0.04 = £10.80
　　　　　　　　　　　　　　New pay = £270 + £10.80 = £280.80

Examiner's note Either method will score you 1 mark for the method of finding percentage increase, and 1 mark for the correct answer.

5 0.23 $\frac{3}{8}$, 39%, 0.4

> *Examiner's note* You should have found this easiest if you changed each number into a decimal. You would score 2 marks if it were all correct, and just 1 mark for only having 1 number thought out incorrectly.

6 (a) $£120 \times 0.078 = £9.36$

> *Examiner's note* You score 1 mark for the method of calculating the 7.8%, and 1 mark for the correct answer.

(b) $£120 \times 1.078 \times 1.078 \times 1.078 = £150.32$ (truncated as banks do!)   or
Increased amount after 1 year will be $£120 + £9.36 = £129.36$
Increased amount after 2 years will be £129.36 increased by
$7.8\% = £139.45$ (truncated)
Increased amount after 3 years will be £139.45 increased by
$7.8\% = £150.32$ (truncated)

> *Examiner's note* The most common error made here is to assume that the increase is the same amount of £9.36 each year and just add that on three times.
> You will score 1 mark for realising that you have to recalculate a new increase each year, you also score 1 mark for increasing it the correct number of times and, of course, 1 mark for the correct answer.

7 The reduction is $£435 - £295 = £140$

So the percentage reduction $= \dfrac{140}{435} \times 100 = 32.2\%$ (rounded)

> *Examiner's note* The most common error is to use the selling price on the bottom of the fraction instead of the original price.
> You score 1 mark for finding the right fraction and multiplying by 100, then 1 mark for the correct answer.

8 The numbers in the ratio $21 : 15 : 9$ add up to 45.

Striker (21 goals) gets $\quad \dfrac{21}{45} \times £9\,000 = £4\,200$

Striker (15 goals) gets $\quad \dfrac{15}{45} \times £9\,000 = £3\,000$

Striker (9 goals) gets $\quad \dfrac{9}{45} \times £9\,000 = £1\,800$

> *Examiner's note* You could have worked this out after simplifying the ratio $21 : 15 : 9$, but the answer would be the same.
> You score the marks as, 1 mark for correctly finding the division factor of 45, 1 mark for correctly evaluating at least one of the bonuses correctly, and a final mark for all the bonuses being correctly worked out.

9 There are lots of correct answers that you could have written for each part, here are some of them:
(a) 25 or 36 or 49 or 64 or 81 or 100, etc.
(b) 50 or 100
(c) 45 or 50 or 55 or 60 or 65 or 70, etc.
(d) 53 or 59 or 61 or 67, etc.

> *Examiner's note* You will get 1 mark for each part as long as you do not have any numbers in there that are wrong.

10 $7 \times 10^{23} \div 3 \times 10^5 = 2.33 \times 10^{18}$ seconds
2.33×10^{18} seconds $\div (60 \times 60 \times 24 \times 365) = 7.4 \times 10^{10}$ light years

> *Examiner's note* You will get 1 mark for dividing the distance by the speed to get the time, and you will get 1 mark for correctly changing seconds into years. The final answer will be worth 2 marks, again 1 for the first part and 1 for the second part.

Algebra

SOLUTIONS TO REVISION ACTIVITY

1 (a) $x = 1$, $y = -5$,   (b) $x = 1.5$, $y = 2.5$

2 (a) $12x^2 - 19x + 5$,   (b) $6x^2 + 5x - 6$,   (c) $2mp + 2pt - 3mt$

3 (a) 4.5,   (b) 1.4,   (c) 2.3

4 (a) $\dfrac{x+2}{2}$,   (b) $\dfrac{x}{b+7}$,   (c) $\dfrac{7t-p}{5}$

5 (a) 4.64,   (b) 15.92,   (c) 4.14

6 (a) $t(3 + 7t)$,   (b) $2m^2(m - 3)$,   (c) $3mp(2p^2 + 3mt)$

7 (a) $(x + 3)(x + 2)$,   (b) $(x - 5)(x - 3)$,   (c) $(x + 5)(x - 3)$

8 (a) $x = -3$ and $x = -4$,   (b) $x = -3$ and $x = 2$

9 (a) $(x + 5)(x - 5)$,   (b) $(t + p)(t - p)$,   (c) $(m + 3)^2$

10 (a) $x > 6.4$,   (b) $t > 8$,   (c) $-6 < x < 6$,   (d) $-1 < x < 0.2$

ANSWERS TO PRACTICE QUESTIONS

1 (a) $0.5 \times 0.75 - 4 = -3.625$

(b) $(0.5 + 0.75) \div -4 = -0.3125$

> *Examiner's note* Care is needed with the negative signs, and remember not just to enter each number into the calculator as it comes along – that is a common fault. The scores will be 2 for each part question: 1 mark for trying to use the correct numbers properly and the other mark for ending up with a correct answer.

2 (a) 6

> *Examiner's note* You will score 1 mark for the correct answer.

(b) $5t = 14 - 6 = 8$
$t = 1.6$

> *Examiner's note* You will score 1 mark for getting the 6 correctly moved to the other side of the equation, then 1 mark for the correct answer.

(c) $3x + x = 20 - 6$
$4x = 14$
$x = 3.5$

> *Examiner's note* You will score 1 mark for correctly rearranging the initial equation, another mark for correctly gathering the like terms together, then a final mark for the correct answer.

3 $C = 35n$

> *Examiner's note* Just 1 mark earned here for writing down the correct formula.

4 (a) Since 30 tickets sold $x + y = 30$
From the costs $3x + 4.5y = 123$

> *Examiner's note* You will score 1 mark for each of these two equations.

(b) Getting xs equal gives $3x + 3y = 90$
$3x + 4.5y = 123$
Subtracting top from bottom gives $1.5y = 33$
Dividing 33 by 1.5 gives $y = 22$
Substitute into $x + y = 30$ gives $x = 8$

Answer is: he sold 8 tickets at £3 and 22 tickets at £4.50.

Examiner's note If you didn't get any equations in part (a) this second part would be difficult. You score 1 mark for getting the simultaneous equations to the stage where you can eliminate the x, you then get a mark for subtracting those two equations, with 1 mark for correctly finding y is 22. Then another mark is for substituting $y = 22$ into an equation to give the last mark for $x = 8$.

5 (a) $5n - n > 22 + 8$

$\qquad 4n > 30 \quad \Rightarrow \quad n > 7.5$

(b) 8

Examiner's note In part (a) you will score 1 mark for correctly rearranging the expressions, with another mark for finding the correct solution.

In part (b) you will get just 1 mark for getting the correct answer.

6 $-9 < x < 9$

Examiner's note The most common mistake made is to forget all about the negative solution. You will score just 1 mark for giving the positive solution only, whereas if you give the whole solution you will gain 3 marks, one for each side of the inequality and 1 for putting it all together.

7 (a) $(40 \times 5) + (5 \times 5) = £225$

Examiner's note You score 1 mark for correctly substituting the value $t = 5$, and 1 mark for the correct answer.

(b) (i) $t = \dfrac{C - 500}{80}$

(ii) $(900 - 500) \div 80 = 5$

Examiner's note The most common error is to write the answer to part (i) sloppily so that it looks like $C - 500/80$, this often results in the wrong calculation being done in part (ii).

You score 2 marks in part (i): 1 mark for getting to $C - 500$, and 1 mark for using 80 correctly as the bottom number of the fraction.

There are 2 marks available in part (ii): 1 mark for substituting $C = 900$ into even your wrong formula in part (i) and then 1 mark for working this out correctly.

8 $3t(1 + 2t)$

Examiner's note You score 2 marks for the solution as above, but just 1 mark if you only partly factorised to an answer like $3(t + 2t^2)$ or $t(3 + 6t)$.

9 (a) $3x^2 - 12x + 2x - 8 = 3x^2 - 10x - 8$

(b) $3t(2t - 3)$

Examiner's note In part (a) you score 1 mark for correctly expanding, then 1 mark for simplifying to the final answer.

In part (b) there are 2 marks for the correct factorisation as shown, with only 1 mark for a partly factorised solution.

10 (a) Find an expression for the perimeter by adding all the sides

$\qquad (x + 5) + (x - 2) + (x + 5) + (x - 2) = 4x + 6$

Since the perimeter is 24, then $\quad 4x + 6 = 24$

$\qquad\qquad\qquad\qquad\qquad\qquad 4x = 18$

$\qquad\qquad\qquad\qquad \Rightarrow \quad x = 4.5$

Examiner's note You will score 1 mark for adding together all the lengths, 1 mark for simplifying the expression and 1 mark for the correct solution.

(b) Multiply the sides for the area: $(x + 5)(x - 2) = x^2 + 3x - 10$

Hence when the area is $60\,\text{cm}^2$, then $x^2 + 3x - 10 = 60$

$\qquad\qquad\qquad\qquad\qquad\qquad \Rightarrow \quad x^2 + 3x - 70 = 0$

Examiner's note You will score 1 mark for expanding the quadratic, 1 mark for putting it to 60 and 1 mark for showing how this rearranges to the final solution.

(c) Solve the quadratic $x^2 + 3x - 70 = 0$
   Factorise to give $(x + 10)(x - 7) = 0$
   Which gives $x + 10 = 0$ and $x - 7 = 0$
                                          $\Rightarrow$ $x = -10$ and $x = 7$
   The only sensible solution to this situation is $x = 7$.

Examiner's note You score 1 mark for attempting to factorise, with 1 mark for correctly factorising. You then will score 1 mark for ending up with the correct single solution.

11 (a) $F = 2C + 30$
   (b) (i)   166
       (ii) 19

Examiner's note There are 2 marks in part (a): 1 mark for the use of 2C and the other mark for finishing it off correctly.
   In part (b) there is 1 mark for each correct answer

3

Graphs

SOLUTIONS TO REVISION ACTIVITY

1 (a) $7\frac{1}{2}$ minutes,   (b) $54\,°C$
2 See Fig. 120.

(a)
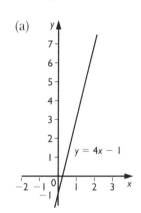
y = 4x − 1

(b)
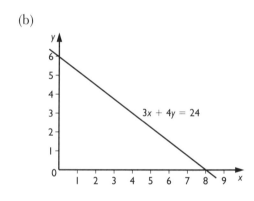
3x + 4y = 24

Fig. 120

(c)
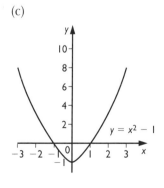
y = x² − 1

(d)
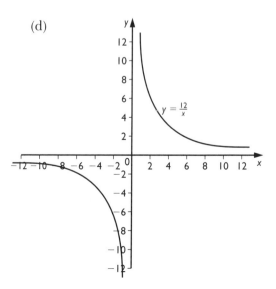
$y = \frac{12}{x}$

3 They are straight lines.

4 (a) 3,   (b) 2,   (c) $-\frac{1}{3}$

5 the speed

6 See Fig. 121.

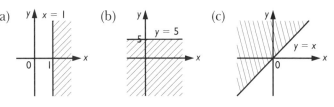

Fig. 121

(a) $x = 1$ (b) $y = 5$ (c) $y = x$

ANSWERS TO PRACTICE QUESTIONS

1 (a) 54 °F,   (b) 24 °C,   (c) 27 °F

> *Examiner's note* You must be as accurate as you can be from the graph, but within 1 millimetre of the correct reading. You will score 1 mark for each correct answer.

2 (a) 10.20, having travelled about 7 miles.

(b) Travelled 32 miles in half an hour, that is 64 mph.

(c) For both the first leg and the last leg we see the car has travelled 35 miles in half an hour, so that is a maximum speed of 70 mph.

> *Examiner's note* It's important to read as accurately as you can, but average speeds are best worked as 'how far would it travel in one hour?'.
>   You would score 2 marks for part (a), 1 mark for each part.
>   You would score 2 marks in part (b) if you got the answer right, but if you did not, then you could still gain 1 mark by stating a non-standard speed.
>   In part (c) the correct answer will again score 2 marks, with 1 mark for an incorrect answer but evidence that you had found some speeds correctly.

3 (a) *Examiner's note* You will score 2 marks for plotting all the points correctly, but lose a mark for any error in the plotting. You must be less than 1 millimetre out to be sure of being correct. You will then score another mark for drawing a straight line through all the points; this line must be drawn with a ruler since any lumps or kinks in it will lose the mark.

(b) (i) £110,   (ii) £55,   (iii) 540

> *Examiner's note* You will score 1 mark for each point correctly read from *your* graph, as long as your reading is less than 1 millimetre out.

(c) Because of the standing charge made even if you use no units.

> *Examiner's note* You will score 1 mark if your comment is about the standing or fixed charges.

4 (a) *Examiner's note* You score 2 marks for plotting the points (lose 1 for any error), and you score another mark for joining the points with a ruled, straight line.

(b) (i) 32 °C,   (ii) 64 g

> *Examiner's note* You score 1 mark for each of these answers.

(c) You can state that b is the point at which the line cuts the vertical axis, $b = 41$, and that a is the gradient of the line. Create a right-angled triangle with any part of this line being the hypotenuse. This should give a gradient about $20/50 = 0.4$, hence $a = 0.4$ and $b = 41$.

> *Examiner's note* You needed to recognise the general formula for a straight line as $y = mx + c$ where m is the gradient and c is the y-axis intercept.
>   You will score marks as: 1 mark for giving b as 41, and 2 marks for finding a as 0.4 (1 mark is for finding the gradient).

(d) You now have the equation $m = 0.4t + 41$, so when $t = 83$
$$m = 0.4 \times 83 + 41 = 74.2\,°\text{C}$$

Examiner's note You could have rounded off the answer to 74, and still scored both marks. You score 1 mark for substituting $t = 83$ into your equation and another mark for the correct answer.

5 (a) You should have drawn two straight lines.

Examiner's note You score 2 marks for each line. If the line is wrong but you have plotted at least one correct point you will score 1 mark.

(b) Your shading should be as shown in Fig. 122.

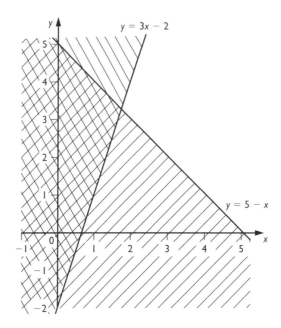

Fig. 122

Examiner's note You score 1 mark for each region correctly shaded.

6 *Examiner's note* You score 1 mark for shading in the correct side of the line, 'on top' of $y + 5x = 100$

7 (b) The intersection gives the solution of the simultaneous equations: $x = 0.6$ and $y = 1.2$. Hence fish and chips cost $60\text{p} + £1.20 = £1.80$.

Examiner's note In part (a) you score 2 marks for each line being correctly drawn. In part (b) you score 1 mark for each of x and y, and then another mark if you give the correct total of £1.80.

8 (a) The table should be completed as

x	-2	-1	0	1	2
y	-10	-2	0	2	10

Examiner's note You score 2 marks for the table, losing a mark for any error.

(b) *Examiner's note* You score 2 marks for plotting the points, (lose 1 for any error), and another mark for joining the points with a smooth curve.

(c) Draw the line $y = 4$ on the graph and find the x ordinate of the intersection. This should be about $x = 1.4$.

Examiner's note You will score 1 mark for showing the line $y = 4$ and another mark for reading off your x ordinate.

9 (a) The table should be completed as

x	1	2	3	4	5	6
y	6	3	2	1.5	1.2	1

Examiner's note You score 2 marks for the table, losing a mark for any error.

(b) *Examiner's note* You score 2 marks for plotting the points (lose 1 for any error), and another mark for joining the points with a smooth curve.

(c) The line should be a ruled, straight line.

Examiner's note This will score 1 mark for a correct answer.

(d) Gradient $= \dfrac{\text{Increase in } y}{\text{Increase in } x} = \dfrac{5}{2} = 2.5$

Examiner's note You will score 1 mark for the method of calculating the gradient, and 1 mark for calculating it correctly.

(e) $(1.9, 3.1)$

Examiner's note This coordinate must be accurate from *your* diagram and be less than 1 millimetre out. You will score just 1 mark for this being accurate enough from your diagram.

4 Mensuration

SOLUTIONS TO REVISION ACTIVITY

1

	Length	Breadth	Perimeter	Area
(a)	6	4	20	24
(b)	10	5	30	50
(c)	7	3	20	21

2

	Base	Vertical height	Area
(a)	6	8	24
(b)	8	3	12
(c)	18	3	27

3

	Vertical height	Parallel side 1	Parallel side 2	Area
(a)	8	5	6	44
(b)	6	8	4	36
(c)	6	7	11	54

4

	Radius	Diameter	Circumference	Area
(a)	7	14	44	154
(b)	4.2	8.4	26.4	55.4
(c)	3.5	7	22	38.5
(d)	8.9	17.8	56	250

5 (a) 157.5 cm^3, (b) 63 cm^3

6 378 g

7 2.42 g/cm^3

ANSWERS TO PRACTICE QUESTIONS

1 Circumference $= \pi \times$ Diameter $= \pi \times 28 \times 2 = 176\,\text{cm}$ (rounded)

Examiner's note You score 1 mark for correctly substituting into the correct formula, and 1 mark for giving a correct answer.

2 Area $= \pi \times$ Radius$^2 = \pi \times 64 = 201\,\text{cm}^2$ (rounded)

Examiner's note You score 1 mark for correctly substituting into the correct formula, and 1 mark for giving a correct answer.

3 (a) You get 5 rows of 15 which gives 75 discs.

Examiner's note You score 1 mark for finding the 15, and another mark for getting the answer to 75.

(b) $20 \times 60 = 1200\,\text{cm}^2$

Examiner's note You get 1 mark for getting this correct.

(c) Area $= \pi \times 2^2 = 12.57\,\text{cm}^2$ (rounded)

Examiner's note You get 1 mark for correctly substituting into the correct formula and getting the area correct.

(d) The 75 discs will have total area of $(\pi \times 2^2) \times 75 = 942.5\,\text{cm}^2$
The amount left for recycling is $1\,200 - 942.5 = 257.5\,\text{cm}^2$

So percentage recycled is $\dfrac{257.5}{1\,200} \times 100 = 21.5\%$ (rounded)

Examiner's note The most common error is to use the rounded off figure from part (c) for this calculation instead of the accurate figure which ought to have been left in the calculator. Another common error is to use the wrong fraction for the percentage error.
You score 1 mark for correctly getting the total area of the 75 discs, 1 mark for finding the amount used for recycling, 1 mark for setting up the fraction correctly to calculate the percentage used, and 1 last mark for the correct answer.

4 (a) $\pi \times 25 \times 2 = 157\,\text{cm}$

Examiner's note You get 1 mark for correctly substituting into the correct formula and getting the circumference correct.

(b) $(50 \times 100 \times 1\,000) \div (\pi \times 25 \times 2) = 31\,830.989 = 31\,831$ revolutions

Examiner's note The most common errors are in converting the kilometres to centimetres, and using the rounded off answer from part (a) to do the calculation.
You score 1 mark for making a good attempt at changing the kilometres to centimetres, 1 mark for knowing you have to divide the 50 km by part (a) and 1 mark for the correct answer.

5 $4.5 \times 5.8 \times 2.8 = 73\,\text{m}^3$ (rounded)

Examiner's note You score 1 mark for substituting into the correct formula and 1 mark for the answer being correct.

6 $\pi \times 3.5^2 \times 8 = 308\,\text{cm}^2$ (rounded)

Examiner's note You score 1 mark for substituting into the correct formula, 1 mark for having an answer that would round off to the correct one and 1 mark for giving the correct units in the answer. (Note that you sometimes, but not always, get marks for using the correct units in an answer.)

7 $\dfrac{3 \times (30 + 5) \times 10}{2} = 525\,\text{m}^3$

> ***Examiner's note*** You score 1 mark for substituting into the correct formula, 1 mark for the correct answer of 525 and 1 mark for using the correct units.

8 $\pi \times 3^2 \times h = 400$ (note we assume $1\,\text{cm}^3 = 1\,\text{ml}$)

$\qquad\qquad h = 400 \div (\pi \times 3^2) = 14.2\,\text{cm}$

> ***Examiner's note*** You score 1 mark for writing down a correct equation using something like *h* for the height, 1 mark for rearranging this to enable you to work out *h*, and then 1 mark for a suitably rounded off answer.
>
> A suitably rounded off number here would be to 1 d.p. since an answer to the nearest millimetre on a can of drink is most appropriate.

9 The question is really 'is the space missing in the pan less than the volume of the cylinder?'

Space missing in pan $\pi \times 10^2 \times (13 - 11) = 628.3\,\text{cm}^3$

Volume of cylinder $\pi \times 3.8^2 \times 12 = 544.4$

There is enough space in the pan so, no, the water will not rise above the pan and spill out.

> ***Examiner's note*** You will score 2 marks for calculating the volume of the cylinder, 2 marks for considering how much space is left above the current water level (or some other suitable method), and 1 mark for correctly stating 'no' and showing why. Please note that an answer of only 'no' with no working would score nothing at all.

10 (a) Area of the top of the washer $= (\pi \times 1^2) - (\pi \times 0.25^2) = 2.945\,\text{cm}^2$

$\qquad\qquad$ Volume $= 2.945 \times 0.2 = 0.589\,\text{cm}^3$ (rounded)

> ***Examiner's note*** The common errors here are not getting the units all the same: you need to be working in centimetres or millimetres, but not both (centimetres lead better into part (b)).
>
> You score 1 mark for demonstrating that you can use the formula for the area of a circle, 1 mark for a good method of finding the area of the face of the washer, and 1 mark for finding its volume.

$\quad$ (b) Density $=$ Weight $\div$ Volume

$\qquad\qquad\qquad = 103 \div (0.589 \times 100) = 1.75\,\text{g/cm}^3$

> ***Examiner's note*** You score 1 mark for using the correct formula, 1 mark for substituting your part (a) answer into it, and 1 mark for the final correct answer.

5 Similarity and solving triangles

SOLUTIONS TO REVISION ACTIVITY

1 (a) *ABE* is similar to *ACD*,   (b) *PQR* is similar to *TSR*

2 (a) 7.8 cm,   (b) 5.7 cm,   (c) 10.2 cm

3 (a) 7.1 cm,   (b) 4.3 cm,   (c) 5.0 cm,   (d) 10.3 cm

4 (a) 60°,   (b) 45.6°,   (c) 24.4°,   (d) 46.2°

ANSWERS TO PRACTICE QUESTIONS

1 AEC is similar to BDC which gives $\dfrac{EC}{DC} = \dfrac{AE}{BD} \quad \Rightarrow \quad \dfrac{6 + ED}{6} = \dfrac{4.9}{3.5}$

Hence $6 + ED = \dfrac{6 \times 4.9}{3.5} = 2.4\,\text{cm}$

Examiner's note The common mistake in any similar triangle problem is using wrong ratios; there are a lot of different ratios you can use, but you must use corresponding lengths.
   You will score 1 mark for picking out corresponding lengths you can use, 1 mark for setting up an equation which will solve to find the missing length, and 1 mark for the correct answer.

2 $\dfrac{\text{Height}}{30} = \dfrac{500}{65} \quad \Rightarrow \quad \text{Height} = \dfrac{30 \times 500}{65} = 231\,\text{m (rounded)}$

Examiner's note Notice that we can use centimetres mixed up with metres here because the lengths are in a ratio where the same units will cancel each other out.)
   You score 1 mark for using corresponding lengths, 1 mark for setting up an equation with those ratios and 1 mark for the final correct answer suitably rounded off.

3 $AB^2 = 10^2 - (7.5 - 5)^2 = 100 - 6.25 = 93.75$
   $AB = \sqrt{93.75} = 9.7\,\text{m (rounded)}$

Examiner's note The most common errors here are not to recognise that the triangle you need to consider is only the top bit of the building and to add the two squares instead of subtracting them.
   You will score 1 mark for correctly finding the difference in heights of the two walls, 1 mark for substituting correctly into Pythagoras' theorem, 1 mark for finding a square root of your calculation, and 1 mark for suitably rounding off the final answer.

4 (a) The scale is $\qquad\qquad 15 \times 1000 \times 100 : 12$
   Which cancels down to $\qquad\qquad 125\,000 : 1$

Examiner's note The common error is not to change the units correctly.
   You will score 1 mark for putting both units into centimetres and 1 mark for simplifying the ratio as above.

(b) $x^2 = 15^2 + 23^2 = 225 + 529 = 754$
   $x = \sqrt{754} = 27.5\,\text{km (rounded)}$

Examiner's note You score 1 mark for correct use of Pythagoras' theorem, 1 mark for square rooting and 1 mark for a suitably rounded off answer.

5 $PR^2 = 17^2 - 5^2 = 264$
   $PR = \sqrt{264} = 16.2\,\text{m}$

Examiner's note The most common error is to add the squares instead of subtracting them.
   You score 3 marks for a suitably rounded off correct answer.

6 $x^2 = 4^2 + 2.8^2 = 23.84$
   $x = \sqrt{23.84} = 4.88\,\text{m (rounded)}$

Examiner's note You score 3 marks for a suitably rounded off correct answer.

7 It is right-angled if the two small sides squared and added equal the long side squared. So, is $4^2 + 12^2$ equal to 13^2?

$$4^2 + 12^2 = 16 + 144 = 160$$

but $$13^2 = 169$$

The two are not the same, so the triangle cannot be right-angled, Margaret is correct.

> ***Examiner's note*** You have to produce a clear argument for someone else to follow, not just convince yourself.
>   You will score 1 mark by showing evidence of using Pythagoras' theorem, 1 mark for finding the sums of the squares, and 1 mark for a sound argument as to why Margaret is correct.

8 (a) Radius $= 9\,\text{cm} \div 2 = 4.5\,\text{cm}$

   (b) Area of the square $= 9 \times 9 = 81\,\text{cm}^2$

   Area of the circle $= \pi \times 4.5^2 = 63.6\,\text{cm}^2$

   So area of shaded part $= 81 - 63.6 = 17.4\,\text{cm}^2$

> ***Examiner's note*** In part (a) you score just 1 mark for stating the correct answer.
>   In part (b) you score 2 marks for finding the correct area of the circle, 1 mark for subtracting this from 81, and 1 mark for the correct answer.

9 (a) (i)   Area $= \frac{1}{2} \times 12 \times 17 = 102\,\text{mm}^2$

   (ii)   Tan $x = \frac{17}{6} = 2.833$

   (iii) $x = 70.6°$

> ***Examiner's note*** You score 2 marks for part (i), 2 marks for part (ii) and 1 mark for part (iii).

   (b) The smallest side is opposite to the smallest angle. Angle A is the smallest, so the side BC is the smallest side.

   $$\frac{BC}{34} = \cos 49° \quad \Rightarrow \quad BC = 34 \times \cos 49° = 22.3\,\text{cm (rounded)}$$

> ***Examiner's note*** You score 3 marks for a suitably rounded correct answer.

10 (a) The angle of elevation is the angle you look up.

   $$\tan x = \frac{80}{1900} = 0.042\,105\,2 \quad \Rightarrow \quad x = 2.4°$$

   (b) $\dfrac{80}{x} = \tan 11° \quad \Rightarrow \quad x = \dfrac{80}{\tan 11°} = 412\,\text{m}$

> ***Examiner's note*** In both parts (a) and (b) you score 3 marks for a suitably rounded correct answer (total 6).

   (c) The boat has moved $(1\,900 - 412)\,\text{m}$ in 10 minutes, which is $1488\,\text{m}$, which would be $1488 \times 6\,\text{m}$ in 60 minutes, which works out to $8.9\,\text{km/h}$.

> ***Examiner's note*** You score 1 mark for expressing the given distance in the 10 minutes and another mark if you can express this as a speed.

Geometry and construction

SOLUTIONS TO REVISION ACTIVITY

1 (a) acute,   (b) obtuse,   (c) reflex,   (d) right angle

2 (a) Exterior angle $= \dfrac{360}{N}$

   (b) Interior angle $= 180 -$ Exterior angle $= 180 - \dfrac{360}{N}$

3 (a) cuboid,   (b) square-based pyramid
4 They are exactly the same shape and size.
5 See Fig. 123.

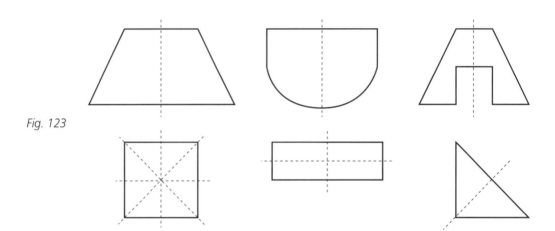

Fig. 123

6 (a) 4,   (b) 2,   (c) 3,   (d) 1,   (e) 2
7 See Fig. 124.

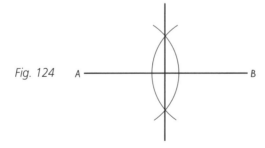

Fig. 124   A ———————————————————— B

8 See Fig. 125.

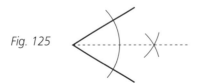

Fig. 125

10 See Fig. 126.

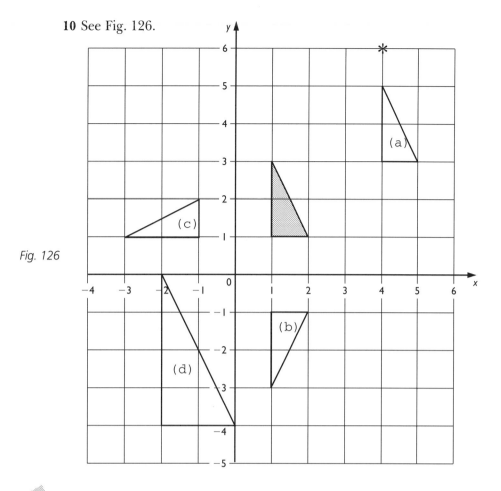

Fig. 126

ANSWERS TO PRACTICE QUESTIONS

1 (a) 40°, alternate angles are equal.

(b) 60°, angles in a triangle add up to 180° and $ACB = 80°$

Examiner's note You will score 2 marks for each part question, 1 mark for the angle and 1 mark for the reason being correct.

2 (a) 90°

Examiner's note You score 1 mark for getting this correct.

(b) (i) There will be 9 equal angles like q all at the centre of the nonagon, so
$q = 360 \div 9 = 40°$.

(ii) $r = 180 -$ Exterior angle (which is the same as q, 40°) $= 140°$.

Examiner's note There are 2 marks for each part question, 1 for a correct method of finding the angle (and there are quite a few), and 1 mark for the correct answer in each case.

3 CDA, because the shape is a parallelogram and so $\angle ABC = \angle ADC$. Also $AB = DC$ and $BC = AD$, hence we have two corresponding sides and the angle between the same, so rule SAS holds, showing them to be congruent.

Examiner's note You would score 2 marks for this question, 1 mark for the correct triangle and another for a valid reason.

4 (a) A reflection in the line $y = x$

Examiner's note Alternatively you could draw the line in, it should go through (0, 0) and (1, 1) etc.
You score 2 marks, 1 mark for saying it's a reflection and 1 mark for identifying the correct line.

(b) and (c) See Fig. 127.

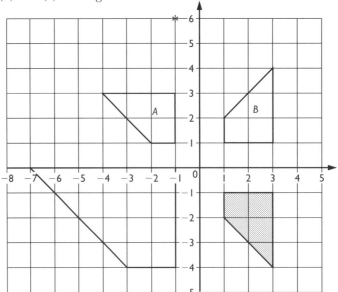

Fig. 127

Examiner's note You will score 2 marks for each part question: 1 mark for attempting the right type of transformation and 1 mark for being accurate.

5 See Fig. 128. The distance to the tree is $2.1\,\text{cm} \times 10 = 21\,\text{m}$.

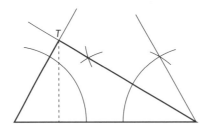

Fig. 128

Examiner's note You should have constructed two 60° angles, and bisected one of them for the 30°.

You score 2 marks for an accurate construction of a 60° angle, 2 marks for an accurate bisection of one of the angles and 2 marks for correctly finding the distance the tree is away from the baseline. In each case you would lose 1 mark if the construction was not accurate.

6 See Fig. 129.

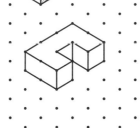

Fig. 129

Examiner's note You score 3 marks for a complete and accurate diagram.

7 Examples are: $4 \times 3 \times 3$ or $12 \times 3 \times 1$ or $6 \times 6 \times 1$ or $2 \times 2 \times 9$

Examiner's note You score 2 marks for a reasonable sketch of a cuboid that looks in proportion to the measurements you have given.

8 (a) 8 possible ways.
  (b) There will be 4 ways without turning the glass round, so if you turn the glass round that will give you $4 \times 2 = 8$ ways.

Examiner's note You will score 1 mark for the answer 8 in part (a). In part (b), you will score 1 mark for a valid reason.

9 4 planes of symmetry.

Examiner's note You score 1 mark for getting this correct.

10 See Fig. 130.

Fig. 130

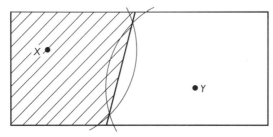

Examiner's note You score 2 marks for correctly constructing the perpendicular bisector of the line *XY*, and another mark for shading in the correct side of the bisector.

11 (a) Has two sides the same length and two angles are equal.
  (b) Has all the sides the same length and all the angles are 60°.
  (c) Has opposite sides parallel and the same length, opposite angles are equal.
  (d) Has a pair of opposite sides parallel.

Examiner's note You score 1 mark for each correct description of the properties of the shapes and 1 mark for each correct drawing. (Your diagrams should look like the Figs on pages 50–1 earlier.)

12

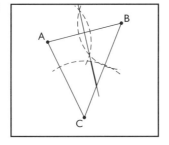

Examiner's note You score 2 marks for the perpendicular bisector of AB, 1 mark for the arc with centre C and 1 mark for correctly identifying the line along which the mast has to be built.

Probability and statistics

SOLUTIONS TO REVISION ACTIVITY

1 (a) mode,   (b) median,   (c) mean
2 There are many correct answers to this question, the following answers are examples:
  (a) 1, 2, 3, 3, 3   (3 is the most frequent)
  (b) 1, 2, 4, 6, 9   (4 is in the middle)
  (c) 2, 3, 4, 5, 11   (all 5 numbers add up to $5 \times 5 = 25$)

3 See Fig. 131.

Fig. 131

4 (a) 36, (b) 28, (c) 45, (d) 17

5 (a) $\frac{4}{12} = \frac{1}{3}$, (b) $\frac{8}{12} = \frac{2}{3}$, (c) $\frac{1}{3} \times \frac{1}{3} = \frac{1}{9}$,
  (d) $\frac{4}{12} \times \frac{3}{11} = \frac{12}{132} = \frac{1}{11}$, (e) $\left(\frac{4}{12} \times \frac{3}{11}\right) + \left(\frac{8}{12} \times \frac{7}{11}\right) = \frac{12}{132} + \frac{56}{132} = \frac{68}{132} = 0.52$

ANSWERS TO PRACTICE QUESTIONS

1 (a) 12, (b) 11, (c) 10.4, (d) 5

Examiner's note The most common errors are to get the different averages mixed up. You score 1 mark for each correct answer.

2 (a) $\frac{26}{100}$ or 0.26 or 26%

Examiner's note One of these correct answers scores 1 mark.

(b) $\frac{58}{100} \times 360 = 209$ (rounded)

Examiner's note You score 2 marks for the correctly rounded answer.

3 (a) $40 \leqslant x < 50$

Examiner's note You score 1 mark for this correct answer.

(b) $(10 \times 16) + (25 \times 21) + (35 \times 28) + (45 \times 38) + (55 \times 17)$
$+ (80 \times 3) = 4\,550$
Estimated mean $= 4\,550 \div 123 = 36.99 = 37$

Examiner's note You score 1 mark for the correct method of using the halfway marks of each group, 1 mark for using these to estimate the total of all students' correct spellings, 1 mark for dividing this total by 123 and 1 mark for the correct, rounded answer.

4 (a) (i) $108 \div 4 = 27$
   (ii) Angle of hot meal $= 360 - (50 + 90) = 220°$
       Number $= \frac{220}{360} \times 108 = 66$ students

Examiner's note You score 2 marks in part (i), and in part (ii) you score 1 mark for calculating the 220, 1 mark for the method of using the fraction $\frac{220}{360}$ and 1 mark for the correct answer.

(b)

	Tally	Total
Hot meal		
Sandwiches		
Quick snack		
Others		

Examiner's note You will score 1 mark for giving the options suggested (you should have included 'others') and 1 mark for giving space for the tallies.

5 (a) That the older you are, the longer it takes you to run the marathon.

Examiner's note You score 1 mark for a correct statement.

(b) Remember to draw a straight line graph, as in Figs. 108 and 109 earlier.

Examiner's note You score 1 mark for using the midpoints of each group, 2 marks for plotting points correctly, 1 mark for using straight lines to join each point and 1 mark for correctly identifying each polygon.

(c) The women's polygon is more spread out than the mens, showing more variety in the times taken.

Examiner's note You score 1 mark for a correct comment.

6 (a) Your diagram should look like one of the graphs shown in Fig. 115 earlier.

Examiner's note You score 2 marks for plotting the points correctly and 1 mark for drawing either a cumulative frequency polygon or a cumulative frequency curve.

(b) (i) 99,   (ii) 14

Examiner's note You score 1 mark for part (i), but 2 marks for part (ii).

(c) (i) James was more consistent, because he had lower interquartile range.
(ii) Helen would have won more games, her median score was less.

Examiner's note You score 2 marks for each part question, 1 mark for the correct name and 1 mark for a correct reason.

7 He would need to do a count of how many times it has been early over a number of weeks. The number of weeks should be 2 or greater. Then he can estimate a probability by the fraction

$$\frac{\text{Number of times early}}{\text{Total number of times counted}}$$

Examiner's note You score 1 mark for stating a count was necessary, 1 mark for suggesting over two or more weeks, and 1 for showing how he would use his results.

8 (a) No.
(b) Because there are far more tickets available to win than the 16 Ben had.

Examiner's note You score 2 marks if your answer is 'no', and you give a satisfactory reason. However, if your reason is not satisfactory, you score no marks at all.

9 (a)

6	7	8	9	10	11	12
5	6	7	8	9	10	11
4	5	6	7	8	9	10
3	4	5	6	7	8	9
2	3	4	5	6	7	8
1	2	3	4	5	6	7
	1	2	3	4	5	6

(b) $\frac{3}{36}$ or $\frac{1}{12}$
(c) $400 \times \frac{1}{12} = 33$ (rounded)

Examiner's note In part (a) you score 1 mark for completing the table correctly.
In part (b) you score 2 marks for the correct answer.
In part (c) you score 1 mark for multiplying your answer to part (b) by 400, and 1 mark for a correctly rounded answer (must be a whole number answer).

10 (a) $\frac{15}{20} = \frac{3}{4}$ or 0.75

> *Examiner's note* You score 2 marks for the correct answer.

(b) See Fig. 132.

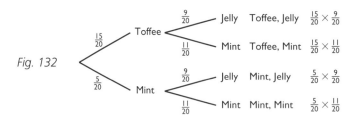

Fig. 132

> *Examiner's note* You will score 3 marks for a fully correct tree diagram, losing 1 mark for any error.

(c) (i) $\frac{5}{20} \times \frac{11}{20} = \frac{55}{400}$ or 0.1375

    (ii) $\left(\frac{15}{20} \times \frac{11}{20}\right) + \left(\frac{5}{20} \times \frac{9}{20}\right) = \frac{210}{400}$ or 0.525

part IV
Timed practice papers with answers

These three papers have been created to give you more examination question practice, but under examination conditions. Each paper should be attempted in a time of 1 hour 30 minutes.

Give yourself the time and the quiet to practise your examination technique. Just as in the real examination, you may get stuck on a question, in which case move on to another problem and come back to that one later.

After completing these practice papers, you can turn to the outline answers at the end of each paper to check how you have done.

These three papers contain material at the Intermediate Level, which might also be encountered at the Higher Level. A separate Exam Practice Kit covers Higher Level materials only.

Grading yourself

After marking your exam practice paper you can grade yourself using the following guidelines. (Note that these scores will not guarantee the suggested grades, but it will give you some clue as to how you are progressing.)

Score 0–14 grade U   You definitely need a lot more thorough revision and learning.

Score 15–19 grade E   You need to do a lot more learning and revising.

Score 20–31 grade D   You are getting close to the better grades, so keep revising and practise more questions.

Score 32–44 grade C   You have mastered at least half of what is to be asked of you, but don't relax – you need to try to learn those parts of the syllabus that you are still getting wrong.

Score 45–64 grade B   Well done, all that revision is paying off, you just need to consolidate and look forward to the exam!

Practice paper 1

1 (a) Bottles of pop cost 29p each. Estimate the cost of 123 bottles.
Show how you obtained your estimate.

....

.... *(2 marks)*

(b) Without using a calculator, find the exact cost of 123 bottles of pop at 29p each.
(You must write down enough working to show you did not use a calculator.)

....

....

.... *(2 marks)*

2 In January 1997 there were an estimated 4 000 puffins on an island.
Owing to pollution, it is predicted that their number will decrease by 15% each year.
(a) How many will be left by January 1998?

....

....

.... *(2 marks)*

(b) By which year will the number first be less than 2 000?

....

....

....

.... *(3 marks)*

3 (a) Express 252 as a product of powers of its prime factors.

....

.... *(1 mark)*

(b) What is the lowest number which 252 must be multiplied by to become a square number?

.... *(1 mark)*

4 Solve the equation $4(x - 1) = 5(x + 2)$.

....

....

....

.... *(3 marks)*

5 Solve the following simultaneous equations

$$5x - 2y = 15$$
$$6x + 2y = 7$$

....

....

....

....

.... *(4 marks)*

6 Rebecca walked from home to the library. She stopped to call on her friend with whom she went to the library. She then returned home. The travel graph of her journey is shown in Fig. 133.

Fig. 133

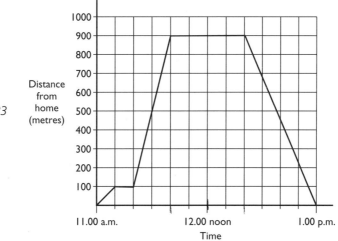

(a) At what time did Rebecca leave her friend's house?

.... *(1 mark)*

(b) How far from the library did Rebecca first stop?

.... *(1 mark)*

(c) How many minutes did she stop at the library?

.... *(1 mark)*

(d) At what average speed (km/h) did Rebecca walk back home from the library?

....

.... *(2 marks)*

7 Gareth is rolling a wheel along the pavement. The wheel has a diameter of 45 cm.
(a) What is the circumference of the wheel?

....

.... *(2 marks)*

(b) What is the minimum number of complete turns the wheel must make to cover a distance of 200 m?

....

.... *(3 marks)*

8 Figure 134 shows two vertical lines AB and CD of lengths 10 m and 4 m. BFD is a horizontal line, where $FD = 6$ m. E is the intersection of AD and BC.

Fig. 134

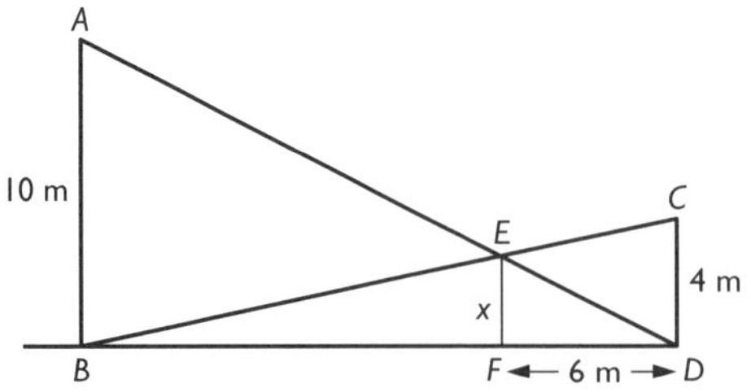

A

10 m

C

E

4 m

x

B

F ◄— 6 m —► D

(a) Write down a triangle that is similar to triangle BEF.

.... *(1 mark)*

(b) Calculate the height marked x.

....

....

.... *(5 marks)*

9 Ville is 18 km due North of Barrusea. Damelle is 29 km due East of Ville.
  (a) Draw a sketch to show the relative positions of Ville, Barrusea and Damelle.

(2 marks)

  (b) Write down the three-figure bearing of Damelle from Barrusea.

....

....

.... *(3 marks)*

  (c) Calculate the direct distance from Barrusea to Damelle.

....

....

.... *(3 marks)*

10 A regular decagon has ten sides. One side of the decagon has been extended to form angle θ (see Fig. 135).

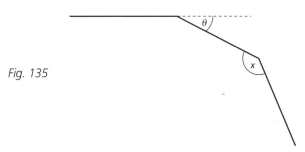

Fig. 135

(a) Work out the size of angle θ.

....
.... *(2 marks)*

(b) Work out the size of angle x.

....
.... *(2 marks)*

11 Look at Fig. 136.

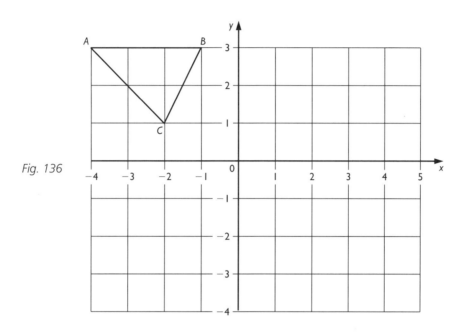

Fig. 136

(a) Write down the coordinates of point A.

.... *(1 mark)*

(b) Rotate triangle ABC 90° anticlockwise about $(0, 0)$. Label this
   triangle P.   *(2 marks)*
(c) Reflect triangle ABC in the y-axis. Label this triangle Q.   *(2 marks)*
(d) Which transformation maps triangle P onto triangle Q?

.... *(2 marks)*

12 (a) Draw in all the lines of symmetry on the shape given in
       Fig. 137.   *(2 marks)*

Fig. 137

(b) State the order of rotational symmetry of Fig. 138.

Fig. 138

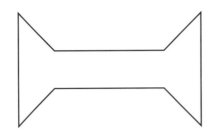

.... *(1 mark)*

(c) How many planes of symmetry does a cuboid have?

.... *(1 mark)*

13 The number of goals scored by 74 football teams were recorded one Saturday.

Number of goals	0	1	2	3	4	5
Number of teams	6	23	29	11	3	2

(a) Write down the modal number of goals scored.

.... *(1 mark)*

(b) Calculate the mean number of goals scored.

....

.... *(3 marks)*

14 This cutting was taken from a local newspaper.

**The under 30s are confident to use computers,
while the over 60s try never to use them!**

Design a questionnaire you could use to see if the statement is true.

....

....

....

....

.... *(3 marks)*

Total 64 marks

OUTLINE ANSWERS

1 (a) $120 \times 30p = 3\,600p = £36$

> **Examiner's note** You get marks for rounding to something to make the calculations easy, hence change the 29 to 30.
> You score 1 mark for suitable rounding and 1 mark for a good approximation.

(b)   123
    ×29
  1 107
  2 460
  3 567   Answer will be £35.67

Examiner's note You will only get any marks if you show how you have calculated without a calculator, so those extra 'carry' numbers are useful to put in.

You score 1 mark for showing how to multiply this way and 1 mark for the correct answer.

2 (a) $4\,000 \times 0.85 = 3\,400$ or 15% of $4\,000 = 600$

Number of puffins now $4\,000 - 600 = 3\,400$

Examiner's note You score 1 mark for either method of reduction being correct, with 1 mark for the correct answer.

(b) You have to do a search involving reducing year by year to find the right number of years.

In January 1998 there will be $3\,400$ puffins

In January 1999 this will be reduced by 15% to $2\,890$

In January 2000 this will be reduced by 15% to $2\,456.5$ (we don't round yet)

In January 2001 this will be reduced by 15% to $2\,088.025$

In January 2002 this will be reduced by 15% to $1\,774.8213$

At last we have a figure less than $2\,000$, so the year will be 2002.

Examiner's note The common mistake is to use the same reduction of 600 puffins every year, or to just write down a year with no evidence to show how it was found.

You score 1 mark for knowing the reductions have to change each year, 1 mark for the type of search shown here to get an answer, and then 1 mark for the correct answer.

3 (a) $2^2 \times 3^2 \times 7$

(b) From the answer to part (a) we can see that if we had the number $2^2 \times 3^2 \times 7^2$ then we would have a square number $(2 \times 3 \times 7)^2$. So we need only to multiply by 7.

Examiner's note You will score 1 mark for part (a) being correct, and 1 mark for finding the number 7 as the answer in part (b).

4 Expand to get $4x - 4 = 5x + 10$

Simplify to get $-10 - 4 = 5x - 4x$

$$-14 = x$$

Examiner's note You need great care with the negative signs, especially when moving numbers around. Remember, when moving an expression from one side to the other, make it do the opposite job.

You will score marks as: 1 mark for correctly expanding out both brackets, 1 mark for correctly gathering either the *x*s or the numbers, then 1 final mark for getting the answer correct.

5 Add the two equations to get $11x = 22$ $\Rightarrow$ $x = 2$

Substitute $x = 2$ into one of the other equations to find that $y = -2.5$

Examiner's note You will score 1 mark for adding the two equations and 1 mark for getting $x = 2$. You will score 1 mark for substituting $x = 2$ into one of the other equations, and 1 mark for getting *y* correct.

6 (a) 11.20 a.m.,   (b) 800 m,   (c) 40 minutes

Examiner's note Each of these responses will score 1 mark.

(d) 900 metres in 40 minutes $\Rightarrow$ 450 metres in 20 minutes

$\Rightarrow$ $1\,350$ metres in 60 minutes

$\Rightarrow$ 1.35 km/hour

Examiner's note You will score 1 mark for finding a distance linked to a time, then as long as you saw this through to the correct speed in km/h you will score the last mark.

7 (a) Circumference $= \pi \times 45 = 141.4\,\text{cm}$ (rounded)

> ***Examiner's note*** You score 1 mark for correctly substituting into the correct formula, and 1 mark for giving a correct answer.

(b) $200 \times 100 \div 141.4 = 141.4$, which means that the wheel must make a minimum of 142 turns.

> ***Examiner's note*** The most common error here is to forget to change the 200 metres to centimetres or to work this out incorrectly. Another common error is not to read the questions properly and to give the rounded off answer of 141, which is wrong.
>
> You score 1 mark for dividing a changed 200 m by your answer to part (a). You score another mark for getting the correct answer to this calculation, and the final mark is for correctly stating you need to make 142 complete turns.

8 (a) BCD

> ***Examiner's note*** You will score 1 mark for this correct answer.

(b) First you must find BF: $\quad \dfrac{BF}{6} = \dfrac{10}{4} \quad \Rightarrow \quad BF = \dfrac{6 \times 10}{4} = 15\,\text{m}$

Now we can find x: $\quad \dfrac{x}{4} = \dfrac{15}{15 + 6} \quad \Rightarrow \quad x = \dfrac{4 \times 15}{21} = 2.857\,142\,9$

$$\Rightarrow \quad x = 2.86\,\text{m}$$

> ***Examiner's note*** The common mistake is not to realise that you have to find BF first, and instead try to find x straight away. (Triangles EAB and ECD are similar.)
>
> You will score 2 marks for finding the length BF and 2 marks for finding the length x. You can also score 1 mark for suitably rounding off the answer to x to 2 or 3 sig. figs.

9 (a) See Fig. 139.

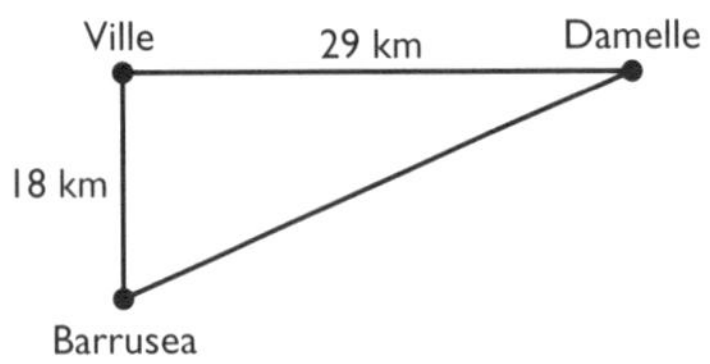

Fig. 139

> ***Examiner's note*** You score 2 marks if this is all correct, 1 mark if you have just two towns placed correctly.

(b) The angle at B is given by $\tan \theta = \frac{29}{18} = 1.6111 \quad \Rightarrow \quad \theta = 58°$
So the bearing is $058°$

> ***Examiner's note*** You score 1 mark for identifying the tan ratio with the correct sides, 1 mark for evidence of dividing the numbers correctly and 1 mark for finding the correct angle.

(c) You could use trigonometry, but you should use Pythagoras here.

$$x^2 = 29^2 + 18^2 = 1\,165$$
$$x = \sqrt{1\,165} = 34.1\,\text{km (rounded)}$$

> ***Examiner's note*** You score 3 marks for a suitably rounded off correct answer.

10 (a) $\theta = 360° \div 10 = 36°$
(b) $x = 180° - 36° = 144°$

> ***Examiner's note*** You will score 2 marks for each part of the question: 1 mark for the method of calculating the angle and 1 for the correct answer.

11 (a) $(-4, 3)$

> ***Examiner's note*** This answer scores 1 mark.

(b) and (c) See Fig. 140.

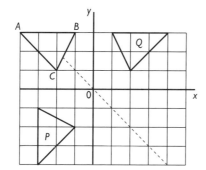

Fig. 140

> **Examiner's note** Both transformations score 2 marks: 1 for the correct type of transformation and 1 for being accurate.

(d) A reflection in the line $y = -x$, or the line could be drawn on the graph as in Fig. 140 (the dotted line).

> **Examiner's note** You score 2 marks: 1 for identifying that it is a reflection and another for indicating the correct line.

12 (a) See Fig. 141.

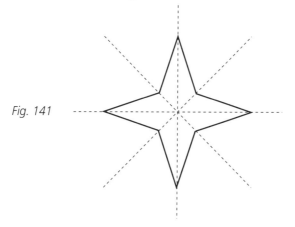

Fig. 141

> **Examiner's note** The common error is to forget the diagonal lines of symmetry. You score 2 marks for the correct answer.

(b) 2,   (c) 3

> **Examiner's note** You score 1 mark for the correct answer in each of parts (b) and (c).

13 (a) 2

> **Examiner's note** You score 1 mark for the correct answer.

(b) $(0 \times 6) + (1 \times 23) + (2 \times 29) + (3 \times 11) + (4 \times 3) + (5 \times 2) = 136$
Hence mean $= 136 \div 74 = 1.8$ (rounded)

> **Examiner's note** The common mistake is to add up the 'goals row' to 15 and divide by that total instead of the 74.
>   You score 1 mark for using an appropriate method for finding the sum of all the goals, 1 mark for dividing this total by 74 and another mark for a correctly rounded answer.

14 Which age group are you in?
Under 30 . . . . .   Between 30 and 60 . . . . . .   Over 60 . . . . . .
Do you ever use computers? . . . .
If you answered 'yes' to the above, are you confident about using computers? . . . .

> **Examiner's note** You score 3 marks, 1 for each relevant acceptable question.

Practice paper 2

1 Ted is calculating the cost of a day-trip to a safari park for his 139 pupils. The cost of entry to the safari park is £12 per person.

(a) Calculate the cost of entry for the 139 pupils *without* using a calculator.

....
....
....
.... *(2 marks)*

(b) For schools, the safari gives a 15% discount on the £12 cost of entry. What is the cost of entry for each pupil?

....
....
....
.... *(2 marks)*

2 Mike draws a plan of his bedroom. He uses a scale of 1 : 40. The bedroom is 8 m long. What will be its length on the plan?
Give your answer in cm.

....
....
.... *(2 marks)*

3 (a) Find the value of 9^3.

.... *(2 marks)*

(b) Find the value of 5^{-3}.

.... *(2 marks)*

4 (a) Show that a solution of the equation $x^2 + x = 10$ lies between 2 and 3.

....
....
.... *(2 marks)*

(b) Use the method of trial and improvement to find this solution of the equation $x^2 + x = 10$. Give your answer to 1 decimal place.

....
....
....
....
....
.... *(4 marks)*

5 Find the whole number values of n that satisfy the inequality $6 \leqslant 4n + 4 \leqslant 30$

....

....

.... *(4 marks)*

6 Given that $y = x^2 + 5$
   (a) Complete the table below.

x	0	1	2	3	4	5	6	7
y				14			41	

(3 marks)

   (b) Plot these points on the grid in Fig. 142 and hence draw the graph of $y = x^2 + 5$. *(3 marks)*

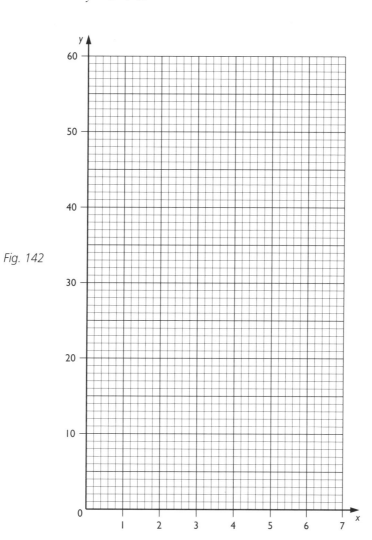

Fig. 142

   (c) Use your graph to find the value of x when $y = 45$.

.... *(2 marks)*

7 A cylindrical tin of soup is 8.5 cm tall and has a base diameter of 7.4 cm (Fig. 143).
   (a) Calculate the area of the base of the tin.

.... *(3 marks)*

   (b) Calculate the capacity of the tin.

.... *(2 marks)*

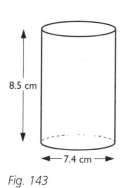

8.5 cm

←—7.4 cm—→

Fig. 143

8 Find the height of a tree which casts a shadow of 1.2 metres, when at the same moment in the same place a woman of height 140 cm would cast a shadow of 50 cm.

....

....

....

.... *(3 marks)*

9 An isosceles triangle has two sides of 8 cm and one of 5 cm. What is the area of the triangle?

....

....

....

.... *(4 marks)*

10

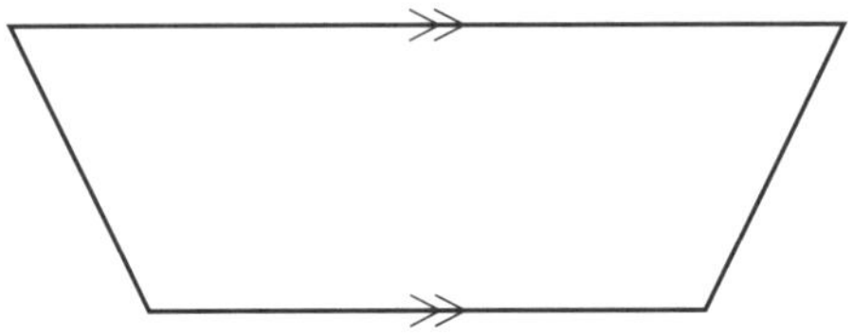

Fig. 144

(a) What is the special name given to the quadrilateral in Fig. 144?

.... *(1 mark)*

(b) Write the letter Y in one obtuse angle in the diagram.   *(1 mark)*

11

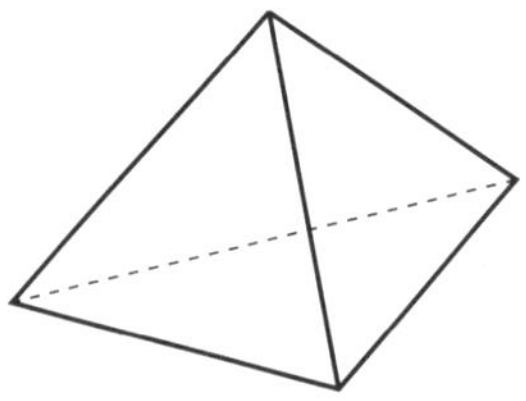

Fig. 145

Sketch a net of the regular tetrahedron shown in Fig. 145.

(3 marks)

12 Two ships X and Y both hear a distress signal from a boat. The positions of X and Y are shown on the map in Fig. 146, which is drawn using a scale of 1 cm to represent 1 km.

   The boat is less than 3 km from ship X and is less than 4 km from ship Y. A helicopter pilot sees that the boat is nearer to ship Y than to ship X.

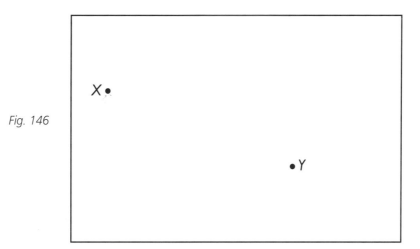

Fig. 146

Draw accurately the region where the boat is to be found.   *(4 marks)*

13 A gardener measures the heights of 100 sunflower plants, correct to the nearest centimetre. This table shows her results.

Height to nearest cm	41–45	46–50	51–55	56–60	61–65
Frequency	11	28	31	16	14

(a) Calculate an estimate of the mean height of the plants in the sample.

....

....

.... *(4 marks)*

(b) Draw a frequency polygon on the grid in Fig. 147 to show the gardener's results.   *(4 marks)*

Fig. 147

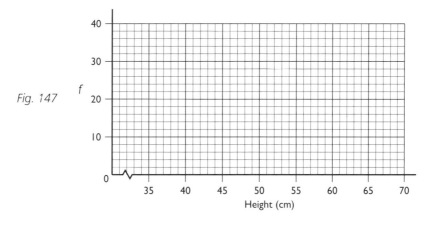

14 Ten people entered a flower exhibition. Their displays were awarded marks by two different judges.

Competitor	A	B	C	D	E	F	G	H	I	J
First judge	91	31	61	17	93	21	7	100	71	44
Second judge	74	29	56	22	73	26	11	88	67	39

The table shows the marks that the two judges gave to each of the competitors.

(a) Draw a scatter diagram on the grid in Fig. 148 to show this information, and on your diagram draw a line of best fit. *(3 marks)*

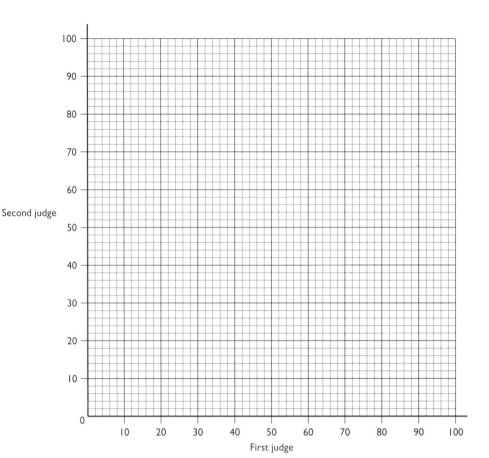

Fig. 148   Second judge

First judge

(b) A late entry was given 65 marks by the first judge. Use your scatter diagram to estimate the mark that might have been given by the second judge.

.... *(2 marks)*

Total 62 marks

OUTLINE ANSWERS

1 (a)   139
       $\times 12$
      ‾‾‾‾‾
        278
      1 390
      ‾‾‾‾‾
      1 668   Answer will be £1 668

Examiner's note You need to show the working for the multiplication as it asks you to do this without a calculator.
   You will score 1 mark for the method of multiplying this way and 1 for the correct answer.

(b) £12 × 0.85 = £10.20   or   15% of £12 = 12 × 0.15 = £1.80
                                  Entry fee = £12 − £1.80 = £10.20

Examiner's note It doesn't matter which way you did the reduction, you would still score 1 mark for the method of finding the percentage reduction and 1 mark for the correct answer.

2 $800\,\text{cm} \div 40 = 20\,\text{cm}$

> *Examiner's note* It was important that you knew to change the units to centimetres first, because that is the biggest cause of error in this type of question.
> You would score 1 mark for dividing by 40 and 1 mark for getting the correct answer with a correct unit of measure.

3 (a) $9 \times 9 \times 9 = 729$, (b) $\dfrac{1}{5^3} = \dfrac{1}{125}$ or 0.008

> *Examiner's note* The marks would be 2 marks for part (a) being correct, and 2 marks for part (b) correct. The answer to part (b) could be left as a fraction for full marks or given as the decimal. If the answer was not correct, then 1 mark might be given for the knowledge that the index -3 meant that it was a fraction.

4 (a) $x = 2$ gives the value of $x^2 + x$ as 6 which is too low
$x = 3$ gives the value of $x^2 + x$ as 12 which is too high
Hence the solution lies between 2 and 3.

> *Examiner's note* At this point you should not be finding the solution, just showing what happens when the you substitute $x = 2$ and 3.
> You will score 1 mark for correctly showing that $x = 2$ is too low a solution, and 1 mark for correctly showing that $x = 3$ is too high a solution.

(b) Trying $\quad x = 2.5$ gives 8.75 $\qquad$ too low
$\qquad\qquad x = 2.7$ gives 9.99 $\qquad$ too low
$\qquad\qquad x = 2.8$ gives 10.64 $\qquad$ too high
We ought to show that $x = 2.75$ gives 10.3125 too high and hence the solution to 1 d.p. is $x = 2.7$.

> *Examiner's note* It is easy to throw marks away here by just doing a trial and error method. You must show a logical improvement from one try to the next, always attempting to narrow the gap that the solution lies within.
> You will score 1 mark for trying a solution between 2 and 3, then another mark for improving that trial. You will score 1 mark for the correct answer and will score 1 mark for showing that $x = 2.7$ is the closest solution, as we have above.

5 Solve each side, so $\qquad 6 - 4 \leqslant 4n \qquad\qquad 4n \leqslant 30 - 4$
$\qquad\qquad\qquad\qquad \Rightarrow \quad 0.5 \leqslant n \qquad\qquad \Rightarrow \quad n \leqslant 6.5$

Putting the two together gives $0.5 \leqslant n \leqslant 6.5$, hence 1, 2, 3, 4, 5 and 6.

> *Examiner's note* You will score 1 mark for rearranging the whole expression, 1 mark for finding the solution at each side, and 1 mark for putting it all together for the final solution.

6 (a) The table should be completed as

x	0	1	2	3	4	5	6	7
y	5	6	9	14	21	30	41	54

> *Examiner's note* You score 3 marks for completing this table, losing 1 mark for any error made.

(b) Draw a smooth curve through your points. The intercept on the vertical (y) axis is 5.

> *Examiner's note* You score 2 marks for plotting the points (lose 1 for any error). You score another mark for drawing a smooth curve.

(c) 6.3

> *Examiner's note* If you had the right answer (or less than 0.1 out), you would score 2 marks. If your answer is wrong but you have shown how you found your answer, then you could score 1 mark.

7 (a) $\pi \times 3.7^2 = 43 \, \text{cm}^2$ (rounded),   (b) $43 \times 8.5 = 366 \, \text{ml}$

> *Examiner's note* In part (a) you score 1 mark for correctly calculating the radius, 1 mark for then substituting this into the correct formula and 1 mark for the correct answer.
>
> In part (b) you score 1 mark for correctly multiplying the answers to part (a) by 8.5, and 1 mark for using the correct units in the answer.

8 $\dfrac{\text{Height}}{1.4} = \dfrac{1.2}{0.5} \quad \Rightarrow \quad \text{Height} = \dfrac{1.4 \times 1.2}{0.5} = 3.36 \, \text{m}$

> *Examiner's note* You could keep the lengths given in centimetres if you wish (it makes no difference to the ratios).
>
> You will score 3 marks for the question: 1 mark for using corresponding lengths, 1 mark for setting up an equation you can use to solve and 1 mark for the correct answer.

9 A diagram will help (Fig. 149).

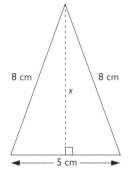

Fig. 149

The dotted line of symmetry gives us a right-angled triangle, base length 2.5 cm.

The height of the triangle x is given by $x^2 = 8^2 - 2.5^2 = 57.75$
$$\Rightarrow \quad x = \sqrt{57.75}$$

The area of the triangle is found by $\frac{1}{2} \times 5 \times \sqrt{57.75} = 19 \, \text{cm}^2$ (rounded)

> *Examiner's note* The common error is to use the 8 as the vertical height of the triangle and simply work out $\frac{1}{2} \times 5 \times 8$.
>
> You score 1 mark for a correct substitution into Pythagoras' theorem, 1 mark for finding the height (either as a number or as a root), 1 mark for the correct use of $\frac{1}{2}bh$ and 1 mark for a suitably rounded answer.

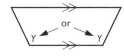

Fig. 150

10 (a) Trapezium

(b) Either one of the two angles indicated in Fig. 150 should be labelled Y.

> *Examiner's note* You score 1 mark for each part question which is correct.

11 See Fig. 151. This is only one of a number of possible correct answers.

> *Examiner's note* You score 3 marks if the net looks like it will work to produce the tetrahedron. You score only 1 mark if all the triangles are obviously not equilateral.

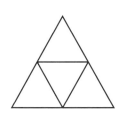

Fig. 151

12 See Fig. 152.

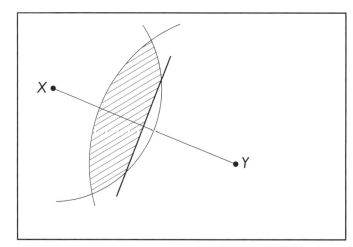

Fig. 152

> *Examiner's note* You score 2 marks for constructing the perpendicular bisector of XY, 1 mark for the correct arcs drawn from centres X and Y and 1 mark for correctly identifying the final region where the boat is.

13 (a) $(43 \times 11) + (48 \times 28) + (53 \times 31) + (58 \times 16) + (63 \times 14) = 5\,270$
Estimated mean $= 5\,270 \div 100 = 52.7\,\text{cm}$

Examiner's note You score 4 marks for a correct answer.

(b) See Fig. 153.

Fig. 153

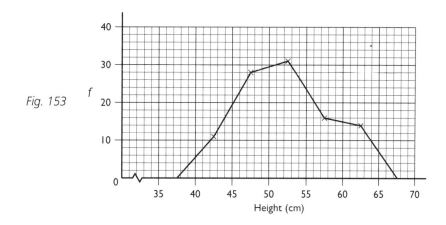

Height (cm)

Examiner's note You score 1 mark for using the midpoints of the groups to plot, 2 marks for correctly plotting all the points and 1 mark for joining up the points with straight lines.

14 (a)

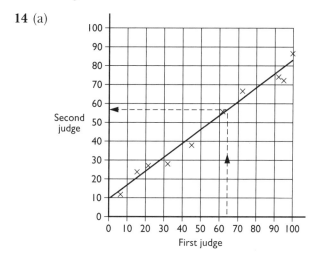

First judge

Examiner's note You score 2 marks for all the points being plotted correctly and 1 mark for a good straight line of best fit.

(b) 57

Examiner's note You score 2 marks for the correct reading from your line of best fit. If you didn't read your graph correctly but you indicted you were trying to use the line of best fit where the first judge gave 65 then you would score 1 mark.

Practice paper 3

1 Charles wins £150 000 on the lottery. He gives £54 000 of this to charity. What percentage is this?

....

....

.... (2 marks)

2 (a) Gillian walked to work at an average speed of 6 km/h. She took 20 minutes for the journey. What distance did she walk to work?

....

....

.... (2 marks)

(b) Peter cycled 4.5 km to work. It took him 20 minutes to travel to work. Calculate his average speed in km/h.

....

....

.... (2 marks)

3 (a) Write each of the following numbers in standard form.
   (i) 37 000 000

.... (2 marks)

   (ii) 0.000 28

.... (2 marks)

(b) Find, in standard form, the value of
   (i) $(5.2 \times 10^{-5}) \times (9.1 \times 10^{12})$

.... (2 marks)

   (ii) $(4.3 \times 10^{-2}) \div (6.73 \times 10^{3})$

.... (2 marks)

4 A rocket is fired vertically upwards with velocity u metres per second. After t seconds the rocket's velocity, v metres per second, is given by the formula

$v = u + gt$ (g is a constant)

(a) Calculate v when $u = 100$, $g = -9.8$ and $t = 8$.

....

....

.... (2 marks)

(b) Calculate t when $u = 89.5$, $g = -9.8$ and $v = 32$.

....

....

.... (3 marks)

5 (a) Factorise fully the expression $2\pi r^2 + 2\pi rh$.

....
.... *(2 marks)*

(b) $Q = T(M - H)^2$. Express M in terms of Q, T and H.

....
....
.... *(3 marks)*

6 Figure 154 shows the graphs of the equations $y = 3x + 1$ and $x + y = 10$.

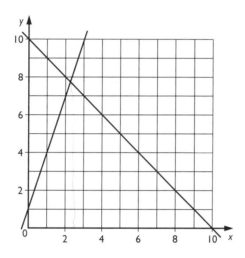

Fig. 154

Use the diagram to solve the simultaneous equations

$$y = 3x + 1$$
$$x + y = 10$$

.... *(2 marks)*

7 Figure 155 shows a running track. AB and DE are parallel and straight. They are each of length 50 metres. BCD and EFA are semicircular. They each have a diameter of length 30 metres.

Fig. 155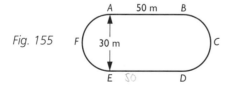

(a) Calculate the perimeter of the track.

....
.... *(3 marks)*

(b) Calculate the total area inside the track.

....
.... *(3 marks)*

8

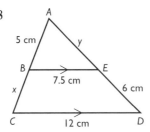

Fig. 156

(a) State which two triangles in Fig. 156 are similar.

.... *(1 mark)*

(b) Calculate the lengths of x.

....
....
.... *(3 marks)*

(c) Calculate the length of y.

....
....
.... *(3 marks)*

9 Figure 157, PQR is a right-angled triangle. PQ is of length 17 cm and QR is of length 14 cm.

(a) Calculate the length of PR.

....
....
.... *(3 marks)*

(b) Calculate the size of angle PQR.

....
....
.... *(3 marks)*

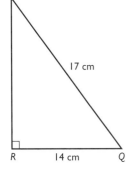

Fig. 157

10

Fig. 158

The triangle ABC in Fig. 158 is translated by the vector $\begin{pmatrix} 2 \\ 1 \end{pmatrix}$ onto $A_1B_1C_1$.

What are the coordinates of C_1?

.... *(2 marks)*

11

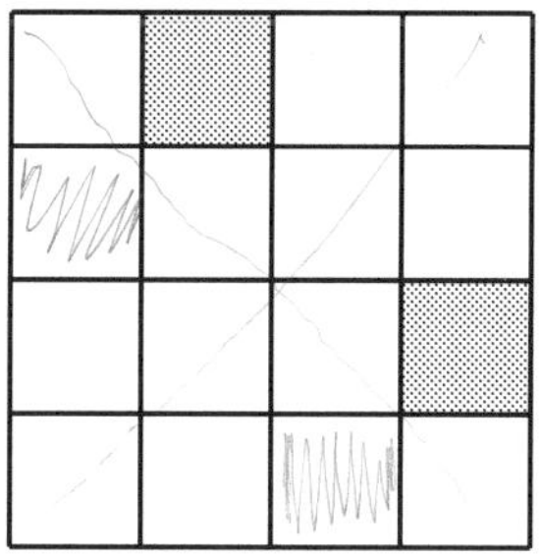

Fig. 159

Figure 159 shows a grid of 16 squares with two squares shaded.
(a) (i) How many lines of symmetry does the diagram have?

.... *(1 mark)*

(ii) State the order of rotational symmetry of the diagram.

.... *(1 mark)*

(b) Shade in two more squares so that the diagram only has two lines of symmetry.   *(2 marks)*

12

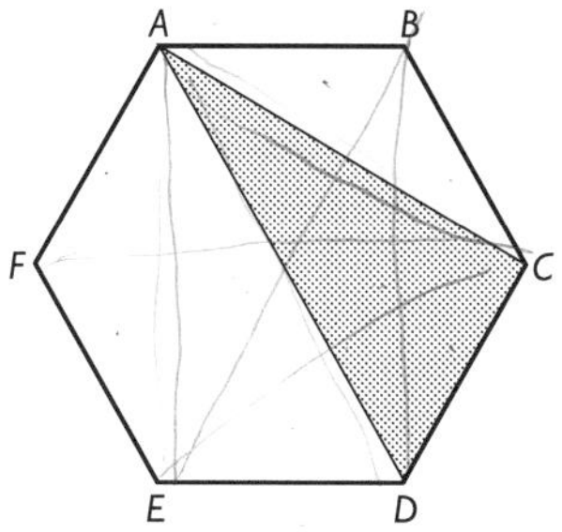

Fig. 160

Figure 160 shows a regular hexagon *ABCDEF*. List all the triangles in the hexagon congruent to *ACD*.

....

.... *(2 marks)*

13 Rita is told to find out which brand of washing powder people prefer. She carries out a survey at a supermarket. The supermarket sells Grubbo, Kleen, Shiftit and Glower washing powders. Devise a table on which Rita can record her results.

....

....

....

....

.... *(2 marks)*

14 A school entered 80 pupils for an examination. The results are shown in the table below.

Mark (x)	$0 \leqslant x \leqslant 20$	$20 < x \leqslant 40$	$40 < x \leqslant 60$	$60 < x \leqslant 80$	$80 < x \leqslant 100$
Number of pupils	2	13	27	27	11

(a) Calculate an estimate of the mean.

....

....

.... *(3 marks)*

(b) Draw a cumulative frequency diagram on the grid in Fig. 161.   *(2 marks)*

Fig. 161

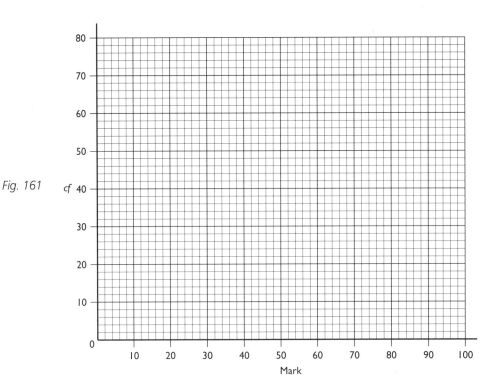

(c) (i) Use your graph to estimate the median mark.

.... *(2 marks)*

(ii) Twelve of these pupils were given a grade A. Use your graph to estimate the lowest mark for which grade A was given.

.... *(2 marks)*

Total 64 marks

OUTLINE ANSWERS

1 $\dfrac{54\,000}{150\,000} \times 100 = 36\%$

Examiner's note You will score 1 mark for knowing how to find a percentage from the fraction and 1 mark for the correct answer.

2 (a) 20 minutes is one-third of an hour, so she would have done $6 \times \frac{1}{3} = 2\,\text{km}$.
   (b) In 1 hour he would have covered $4.5\,\text{km} \times 3 = 13.5\,\text{km/h}$.

Examiner's note You needed to remember the links between distance, time and speed. You would score 2 marks in each part of the question. Full marks if your answers were correct, and just the 1 mark in each part if you were trying to do the right thing but made a simple error in the calculation.

3 (a) (i) 3.7×10^7,   (ii) 2.8×10^{-4}
   (b) (i) 4.732×10^8,   (ii) 6.3×10^{-6}

Examiner's note You will earn 2 marks for each part (8 in total). You will gain 1 mark for the first part of the standard form number and one mark for the second part of 10^n.

4 (a) $100 + -9.8 \times 8 = 21.6$

Examiner's note You will score 1 mark for putting the numbers into the formula correctly, then another mark for getting the answer correct.

   (b) $t = (32 - 89.5) \div -9.8 = 5.87$

Examiner's note Care is needed with those negative signs and you do need to round off your calculator answer to something suitable (like 3 s.f.).

You will score 1 mark for either transforming the formula correctly or showing this in your calculations, then 1 mark for correctly using the correct numbers and 1 mark for the final correct answer.

5 (a) $2\pi r(r + h)$

Examiner's note There are 2 marks for the correct factorisation, with only 1 mark for a partly factorised solution.

   (b) $\dfrac{Q}{T} = (M - H)^2 \;\; \Rightarrow \;\; \sqrt{\dfrac{Q}{T}} = M - H \;\; \Rightarrow \;\; \sqrt{\dfrac{Q}{T}} + H = M$

Examiner's note The square rooting is the biggest problem in this question, you need to show clearly which terms are being square rooted.

You will score 1 mark for correctly moving the T first, then 1 mark for dealing with the square, and 1 mark for the final expression being correct.

6 The solution is found at the point where the two lines cross. Read the coordinates there as $x = 2.2$ (or 2.3) and $y = 7.8$ (or 7.7).

Examiner's note The common mistake is to give only the x coordinate. Notice that because of the scale you are allowed some variance with the answer (although you should notice from the equations that your two numbers should add up to 10).

You will earn 2 marks: 1 for each of x and y.

7 (a) $(\pi \times 30) + (50 \times 2) = 194\,\text{m}$ (rounded)

Examiner's note You score 1 mark for using $(\pi \times 30)$, 1 mark for this method of adding all the lengths together, and 1 mark for the answer being correct.

   (b) $(\pi \times 15^2) + (50 \times 30) = 2\,207\,\text{m}^2$

Examiner's note You score 1 mark for using $(\pi \times 15^2)$, 1 mark for this method of adding both areas and 1 mark for the correct answer.

8 (a) ABE is similar to ACD.

Examiner's note You score 1 mark for getting this correct.

   (b) $\dfrac{x + 5}{5} = \dfrac{12}{7.5} \;\; \Rightarrow \;\; x + 5 = \dfrac{5 \times 12}{7.5} = 8$

$$\Rightarrow \quad x = 3\,\text{cm}$$

   (c) $\dfrac{y + 6}{y} = \dfrac{12}{7.5} \;\; \Rightarrow \;\; 7.5y + 45 = 12y$

$$\Rightarrow \quad 45 = 4.5y$$

$$\Rightarrow \quad y = 10\,\text{cm}$$

Examiner's note You will score 3 marks for each part (b) and (c): 1 for using corresponding lengths, 1 for setting up the equations and 1 for the answers being correct.

9 (a) $PR^2 = 17^2 - 14^2 = 93$

$ PR = \sqrt{93} = 9.6\,\text{cm}$ (rounded)

Examiner's note You will score 3 marks for a suitably rounded answer.

(b) $\cos PQR = \dfrac{14}{17} = 0.8235 \quad \Rightarrow \quad \angle PQR = 34.6°$

Examiner's note You will score 1 mark for correctly identifying the cosine and the two sides in the correct ratio, 1 mark for showing evidence of calculating the cos of the angle and 1 mark for the correct answer.

10 (5, 3)

Examiner's note You score 1 mark for each correct ordinate in the answer.

11 (a) (i) 1,   (ii) 1

Examiner's note You score 1 mark for each correct answer.

(b) The only solution is shown in Fig. 162.

Fig. 162

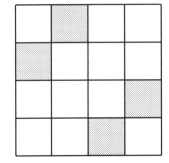

Examiner's note You will score 2 marks for completing the diagram correctly.

12 $BDE, CEF, DFA, EAB, FBC.$

Examiner's note You score 2 marks if they are all correct, if one is wrong you will score just 1 mark.

13

	Tally	Total
Grubbo		
Kleen		
Shiftit		
Glower		

Examiner's note You score 1 mark for listing the 4 washing powders (you might include 'others', which is quite acceptable). You also score 1 mark for there being space devoted to the tallies.

14 (a) $(10 \times 2) + (30 \times 13) + (50 \times 27) + (70 \times 27) + (90 \times 11) = 4\,640$
     Estimated mean $= 4\,640 \div 80 = 58$

Examiner's note You score 3 marks for the correct answer.

(b)

Examiner's note You score 2 marks for plotting the points correctly and 1 mark for drawing either a cumulative frequency polygon or a cumulative frequency curve.

(c) (i) 58,   (ii) 78

Examiner's note You score 2 marks for each correct answer.

LONGMAN
EXAM
PRACTICE
KITS

REVISION
PLANNER

Getting Started   *Begin on week 12*

Use a calendar to put dates onto your planner and write in the dates of your exams. Fill in your targets for each day. Be realistic when setting the targets, and try your best to stick to them. If you miss a revision period, remember to re-schedule it for another time.

Get Familiar   *Weeks 12 and 11*

Identify the topics on your syllabuses. Get to know the format of the papers – time, number of questions, types of questions. Start reading through your class notes, coursework, etc.

Get Serious   *Week 10*

Complete reading through your notes – you should now have an overview of the whole syllabus. Choose 12 topics to study in greater depth for each subject. Allocate two topic areas for each subject for each of the next 6 weeks

No. of weeks before the exams	Date: Week commencing	MONDAY	TUESDAY
12			
11			
10			

Titles Available –

GCSE
Biology
Business Studies
Chemistry
English
French
Geography
German
Higher Maths
Information Systems
Mathematics
Physics
Science

A-LEVEL
Biology
British and European Modern History
Business Studies
Chemistry
Economics
French
Geography
German
Mathematics
Physics
Psychology
Sociology

There are lots of ways to revise. It is important to find what works best for you. Here are some suggestions:

- try testing with a friend: testing each other can be fun!
- label or highlight sections of text and make a checklist of these items.
- learn to write summaries – these will be useful for revision later.
- try reading out loud to yourself.
- don't overdo it – the most effective continuous revision session is probably between forty and sixty minutes long.
- practise answering past exam papers and test yourself using the same amount of time as you will have on the actual day – this will help to make the exam itself less daunting.
- pace yourself, taking it step by step.

WEDNESDAY	THURSDAY	FRIDAY	SATURDAY	SUNDAY

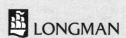